# Born Before Plastic

# Born Before Plastic

*Stories from Boston's Most Enduring Neighborhoods*

VOLUME I

North End, Roxbury,
and South Boston

CITY OF BOSTON    GRUB STREET, INC.

*With special thanks to*

*all of the participants for making this possible*

CITY OF BOSTON
Mayor Thomas M. Menino, Mayor of Boston
Michael Kineavy, Chief of Policy and Planning

COMMISSION OF AFFAIRS OF THE ELDERLY,
    CITY OF BOSTON
Eliza Greenberg, Commissioner
Kaysea Cole, Deputy Commissioner
Eileen O'Connor, Staff Photographer

GRAPHIC ARTS AND PRINTING DEPARTMENT,
    CITY OF BOSTON
Paul Dennehy, Superintendent

GRUB STREET, INC.
Christopher Castellani, Artistic Director,
    Interim Executive Director
Marc Foster, Co-President, Board of Directors
Eve Bridburg, Founder
John LaFleur, Board of Directors
Michelle Seaton, Head Instructor, The Memoir
    Project
Valerie Stephens, Instructor and Coach
Alexis Rizzuto, Head Writing Coach and
    Editor of *Born Before Plastic*
Kerrie Kemperman, Writing Coach and Assistant
    Editor of *Born Before Plastic*
Kali Borrowman, Elisabeth Carter, Cassandra
    Cato-Louis, and Jenny Desai, Volunteer
    Writing Coaches
Whitney Scharer, Associate Director of
    Programming and Development
Sonya Larson, Program Coordinator
Jordan Payne, Memoir Project Intern

Melissa Lotfy, Art Director
Julia Boyles, Design and Production Intern
Mark Robinson, Cover Designer

Bernard A. Margolis, President, Boston Public
    Library

Ed Pignoli and the staff of the Old North Church
    Association
Bill Spain and the Castle Island Association
The South Boston and Grove Hall branches of the
    Boston Public Library

Emily Berl, Photographer

Joann Riley and the Mass Memories and Road Show

Lisa Grace, Grace Video Productions

Pat Bartevian

Grub Street, the City of Boston, and the Memoir
Project are enormously grateful to the following
funders for their generous support: the Llewellyn
Foundation, the Calderwood Writing Initiative
at the Boston Athenaeum, and the Massachusetts
Cultural Council.

ISBN-13: 978-0-615-15208-0

Senior citizens are the foundation on which Boston was built. The people who shared their memories and participated in the *Memoir Project* represent thousands of families who have paved the way for us all. The generation represented in this book believed in hard work and family values, and their tremendous sense of pride will forever shape the history of Boston.

I am hopeful this book will teach future generations about our great city.

I am honored to dedicate this book to Boston's seniors.

With sincere gratitude, I thank you.

Sincerely,

Thomas M. Menino
Mayor of Boston

# *Contents*

What We've Lost

# *Foreword*

It is with great joy that the City of Boston and Grub Street welcomes the first publication of the Memoir Project, *Born Before Plastic,* a book that has literally taken over seventy years to write. We hope this anthology will serve as a lasting testament to the ordinary and extraordinary lives of the authors represented here.

The idea for the Memoir Project was conceived by the Board of Directors at Grub Street in the summer of 2005. They decided to make it a priority to offer writing classes to senior citizens of Boston. The goal of these writing classes was not just to preserve these stories for future generations but to bring seniors together as they practiced their craft.

At the same time, Mayor Thomas M. Menino was looking for ways to offer seniors free programs that were rich in quality beyond traditional health and human services. He saw a need, in particular, to enable older residents of the city to give voice to their thoughts and feelings by putting meaningful events from their lives down on paper.

The two groups came together and inspired each other about the idea. Mayor Menino shaped the Memoir Project by providing locations, recruiting participants, and utilizing community links and resources for the workshops in the North End, Roxbury, and South Boston. Grub Street, which has a national reputation for high-quality writing workshops, then designed a curriculum and hired one of its instructors, Michelle Seaton, to teach the first sessions.

Since then, the Memoir Project has employed a number of teachers, writing coaches, and staff in six Boston neighborhoods. These dedicated mentors have helped nearly one hundred seniors generate and shape their life stories, excerpts of which are on display in this volume.

We are proud of the hard work accomplished by all the members of this dynamic team. The book speaks for itself. We hope you enjoy this trip back in time to a Boston that in some ways no longer exists, and in other ways seems quite familiar.

CHRISTOPHER CASTELLANI
*Artistic Director, Grub Street*

MAYOR THOMAS M. MENINO
*City of Boston*

MARC FOSTER
*Co-President, Grub Street*
*Board of Directors*

ELIZA GREENBERG
*Commissioner on Affairs of*
*the Elderly*

# Notes from the Classroom

That first morning of our first-ever Memoir Project workshop in the North End, the only question was whether anyone would show up. The participants who had signed up for the free four-week workshop on memoir writing had done so tentatively. Marc Foster from Grub Street and Kaysea Cole from the mayor's office had gone to neighborhood senior centers. They put up fliers. They put an ad in the local paper asking for people to give it a try. They spoke to seniors who said that they didn't have any interesting stories to tell, or that writing seemed too hard.

We scheduled the workshop anyway, stood around in a little conference room next to the Old North Church, and hoped. To our relief, and then shock, sixteen people showed up, accepted notebooks and pens, and waited for their first writing exercise. For the next four Tuesdays, the seniors wrote and talked about life before World War II; about immigrating from Italy to Boston; about parents who could not speak English and could not get reliable work, but managed to create a wonderful if precarious home life in their adopted country. At the end of the workshop, everyone was sad. The participants said that they had talked and written about things they hadn't even thought about in over fifty years.

This happened again in South Boston, and again in Roxbury. At first, participants seemed to be humoring us, talking and writing about their lives because we'd asked them to. Over the course of the class, they began to tell each other their stories and ask each other for more information about their stories. They even shushed each other when the class became boisterous, so that they could better hear the person talking or reading aloud from his or her notebook. Participants wanted to know how their experiences varied from their contemporaries'. By the time the class had moved to Roxbury, participants were asking for details about what those in the other neighborhoods had written about. How did their childhoods and their neighborhoods differ from others in Boston? This book is an attempt to answer that curiosity, to give these participants as well as the people of Boston a chance to look into the past and into the intimate histories of different Boston neighborhoods. There are some life experiences that could have happened only in Boston, and in fact, could have happened only in a few city blocks inside of one of these neighborhoods.

What makes this class different from an oral history project is the fact that peers from discrete neighborhoods, in some cases people who have known each other for fifty years, are sharing their life experiences. They aren't sitting alone telling their stories into a tape recorder to a young interviewer anxious to know how the world used to be. They are talking to people who also remember these things. They are talking to peers about past fears and challenges that they may not have shared before with even their closest friends. In the process they are uncovering a texture to past experiences, music, food, and attitudes that they never thought they would remember.

MICHELLE SEATON
*Head Instructor*

# Introduction

You hold in your hand a mosaic of lives, richly colored by individual experiences. In these pieces by those who grew up during the Depression and World War II, you will find a deep sense of history, from techniques for surviving on next-to-nothing ("Make it do, make it last, or make it over") to the sense of sacrifice, civic participation, and solidarity engendered by wartime. You will read stories of a real-life Rosie the Riveter, a soldier shipping out to war while thinking of his wife and child back home, a daughter waiting weeks to hear if her father survived the attack at Pearl Harbor, an uncle coming home from war with hard lessons to teach, a family toasting the safe return of four sons.

But their history doesn't end with the war; citizens soon got down to the business of making a life and rebuilding the country. They fell in love, married and had children, enjoyed social lives, dedicated time to community service. They found meaning through a variety of vocations: as an artist, a barber, a nurse, an interpreter, by joining the Marines, by taking in neglected children. And many took part in the country's next great struggle, fighting the enemy of discrimination within our borders, as a Black Panther, a civil rights activist, by marching on Washington with Martin Luther King, Jr., by demanding equal educational opportunities for their children.

The sense of history also goes back in time as this generation reflects on the strength of its forebears, the parents and grandparents who modeled the values of hard work, education, faith, service, and putting family first.

This is a generation that largely stayed put, contributing to a profound sense of place. In an informal poll of one class, the average number of years lived in their neighborhood was sixty-eight. Many had spent their entire lives—up to eighty-seven years in this case—in one place. Such intimacy with the streets on which they grew up and raised their children is becoming rare. As residents for so many years, they have been witnesses to the changes brought by "progress." Many of the places described here—the North End Beach, Roxbury's Madison Park, the grand train stations like Dudley—exist only in memory and are brought to life in loving and wistful detail: the smells of the local bakery, the taste of ice cream from the local drugstore counter, the sounds of the milkman's bottles clinking, the feel of washing one's face with chips from the iceman's cart on a hot summer day.

Not everyone was so rooted, as immigration to this country and migration to the Northeast from the South and Midwest are also part of many of these writers' lives. New England was a culture shock for some, while it provided new opportunities for others. One Navy wife found travel itself liberating, opening the door to a new way of seeing herself in the world.

Another sense that permeates these stories is that of connectedness to one's neighbors and community. A description common to all three neighborhoods is the memory of adults sitting on front steps socializing while children played games in the streets, of watching out for each other, of sharing. In the North End, if your grandmother was making a pizza, she'd make two and send one to a neighbor. In South Boston, a kid couldn't misbehave in public without being reported to his mother by someone else's mom. In Roxbury, the fishmonger would save the scraps for a mother of fifteen to make stew for her brood. Many seniors lived by my grandmother's saying, "Always keep your house clean, you never know who will come to visit and you must always have your house open for visitors." Her generation did much more visiting than mine.

Tom Brokaw describes the "greatest generation" as being "united not only by a common purpose but also by common values—duty, honor, economy, courage, service, love of family and country, and, above all, responsibility for oneself." Although the authors of this anthology may be separated by as much as twenty years in age, and come from distinct neighborhoods and cultural backgrounds, their stories show how strongly held these common values are. It has been an honor to work with these elders, to witness the strength and nobility, the humor and humility with which they have lived and have written about their lives. We hope you enjoy and learn from this collective portrait of an era, a city, and the people who live there.

ALEXIS RIZZUTO
*Editor*

# Where We're From

# FAMILY IN THE
# GOOD OLD DAYS

## *Patricia Beckles*

IN MY FAMILY we had a cousin, 'Will.' Now, when Will came to town we always ate "high on the hog." Perhaps we didn't eat well the rest of the week but when Will was in town we sure did; you see Will had graduated from high school, gone to college, and become a speaker.

I remember my grandmother and her sister getting ready to go listen to Cousin Will speak. Picture this: two little old ladies, not more than five feet tall, each thin as a rail, all dressed in black, getting dolled up to go see Will. Now, getting dolled up meant taking the white lace off one dress and putting it on another, so no one would know it was the same dress. You know, I never saw my grandmother in anything but black.

Anyway, these two old ladies would clutch one another's arm and go out in traffic to see Cousin Will. They had to cross Tremont Street and there weren't any traffic lights on the corners then, but of course, only a half dozen cars went by in an hour. I never knew until many years later that they sat in the back of the hall to hear Will speak, but never let him know they were there, because by then he had graduated from several colleges

and was very famous, and they were ashamed that they hadn't progressed as he had.

Now, about "cuzzin" Will. He was not a tall man. My dad was six foot four and Cousin Will was not even six feet tall. He always dressed well, with a suit and tie, and always wore shined shoes. He had a very clear voice and pronounced his words with care. He had an air about him that made you think twice about addressing him, although with my grandma, he relaxed and was just family. I was not impressed with him or his titles, I was just glad he had come to visit because I knew we would have a great meal.

Some time later, I asked my grandmother why we hadn't seen Will in a long time, and she said to me, "Kitty," — I don't know why she called me Kitty — but she told me not to mention him anymore, because he had become a communist and if the police knew he was related to us we would all go to jail. Well, honey, you know Will was gone from my mind in a flash. I knew I didn't want to go to jail!

I grew up, but always in the back of my mind I missed the good old days when Will would come to visit. No one explained to me about prejudice, I just knew it was there and it was a fact of life.

Will was the first in our family to finish high school, the first to graduate from several colleges, and to go on to international fame, and yet I was made to feel ashamed of him, because of the pervasive atmosphere of the good old days.

Well, I stand here today proudly to tell you that Cousin Will was my cousin William Edward Burghardt Dubois.

When I think on how Grandma was ashamed that she had not risen as high above her humble beginnings, I am proud to remember that five

*Roxbury, 1910. My grandmother and her sister. W.E.B. Dubois was their first cousin.*

of us first cousins graduated from the Massachusetts Memorial School of Nursing within three years of each other, most getting secondary degrees. One became a headmaster of a local high school, while the others became nurses or teachers. And I wonder what Cousin Will would think of us now!

# MEMORIES OF
# A HAPPY GHETTO

## *Angie DeMinico*

I WAS THE YOUNGEST of four children, born and raised in the North End of Boston. I was born in 1940, so a lot of my memories date back to the 1950s. I would describe the North End as a happy ghetto. I say that because the North End was considered a tenement district. For the most part, we were all in the same boat. Our parents worked very hard. We always had plenty of food and family sit-downs around the supper table, which today is a rarity. We may not have had much, but our parents instilled in us the wonderful values of self-respect, being responsible, hard work, and being nice to neighbors. My mother was all for education. On recommendation of his teacher, my brother went to Boston Latin and Boston College. Despite being known as a ghetto, the North End has produced many professionals—doctors, lawyers, politicians, etc.

I was very happy there myself, and have many fond memories of the neighborhood. I was lucky to be able to go to after-school programs at the North Bennett Street Industrial School. They had cooking, dramatics, piano, and many other classes, along with a game room.

Most of the older folks went to the "bathhouse" for a bath. I suppose I was lucky to have a "stack heater" in our kitchen to heat water and sponge bathe.

When I was twelve or thirteen years old, my mother would send me to buy bread. With the few pennies change, my friends and I would congregate in the apartment building hallways and play a card game we called seven and a half, which today is twenty-one. My mother would scold me for being late and I would tell her I lost the change.

Other times when my mother sent me on errands, being that we lived on the fourth floor, I would go in the first floor hallway and quickly pull the light switch lever on our electrical box. That would signal my mother to send a leather bag on a long rope down the stairwell to send up the package. When I think of that today, I think wow, it's a wonder I didn't get electrocuted.

Another funny story is when my mother used to make raviolis. She would put a large white spread on the bed to place the raviolis to dry. My mother would scold me because I would line them up on both arms and try to carry them. Needless to say, a few fell.

When the summer came, I remember the West End getting their Metropolitan District Commission (MDC) pool first. A whole gang of boys and girls would go and spend the whole day. When I returned home one time, I was burnt to a crisp. Of course it was because I had been in the sun all day, but my mother thought someone must have cursed me. She had an elderly neighbor perform the "evil eye." The neighbor took a basin of water and added drops of oil. Depending on how they fell, I had the "evil eye" — that formula was also used for someone talking about you, bad dreams, etc.

I remember our first television. It was a floor model Motorola TV. Thank goodness we had a large kitchen. My sister and brothers would lie criss-

cross with each other on the floor. As we became teenagers, we petitioned my mother for a room to have friends over to socialize. She bought a hideaway bed, chair, and coffee table, which gave us some semblance of a sitting room.

When I used to go to the Feast of Saint Anthony, my friends and I would go to Pizzeria Regina and pitch in for a pizza, then walk through the feast and purchase a shot glass of seeds and nuts for five cents. When my nieces and nephews were young, the feast was less commercialized than it is today. They recall the confetti falling from the rooftops. After the saint had passed, they would play in the inches of con-

fetti. I can picture them now: all the children half-covered with confetti, whisking it up in the air and having lots of fun. They remember the fifteen minutes of fireworks at noon at the Gas House (or "Gassie"). They remember all the people, especially their "Nonni," hanging out the windows. They also remember the North End when people would sit on their chairs and benches on the hot summer nights speaking broken English and enjoying themselves. Oh, the smell of the pastry and bakery shops!

I cannot speak for the generation today, but from my observance, I would not trade being born and raised in the North End at that time for all the technology and advancement today.

*First Communion,*
*May 1947*

# SATURDAY SCENES

## *Keitha B. Hassell*

I WAS BORN AND RAISED in Roxbury and have many happy memories. Some of my memories include: seeing some of the last horse-drawn wagons that peddlers used; seeing one of the last lamplighters who lit the gas light every night; and watching one of the last blacksmiths use a hammer and anvil in his shop. When I was small I also lived in a house with one radio and one party-line phone, no television, no CDs, no DVDs, no iPods, no air conditioners, and thankfully no cell phones. I was born before plastic!

My sister and I were very fortunate to be the children of two loving, caring parents whom we took for granted until we became adults.

We kids usually looked forward to the weekends because those were the days that we had the most time to spend with our parents and friends. Even though we had special chores on Saturdays, there was still much time left for fun. One ritual chore was sweeping: we lived on the second floor of a three-decker on Hollander Street. Every Saturday, the lady upstairs would sweep down to our floor, then we'd sweep down to the first

floor and out the front door. People were very particular about house cleaning in those days.

I loved to go shopping with my mother on Saturday. It took several hours because she had to go from store to store; there were no big supermarkets then. We would first go to the grocery store, where of course we would walk, as very few people had cars back then. She would order her groceries and then pay one of the teenage boys to deliver them to the house. She would just tell the youngster, "Put the groceries on my kitchen table."

The doors were almost always unlocked so the delivery boy would put the groceries in a box and then in a metal cart, and when he had a full cart he would make his deliveries. During the day one could hear the rumble of metal wheels as they rolled up the streets. When we got home after making all the stops at the fish store, poultry store, fruit market, drugstore, and bakery, our groceries would be on the kitchen table. We never even thought that one of these boys would take anything, and as far as I know my mother never missed a thing. Saturday shopping time was also a way for the women (and children who were with them) to stop along Harold Street or Humboldt Avenue and chat with their friends—people visited and interacted more with their neighbors then.

Another Saturday memory that I have is attending the cricket matches at Franklin Field with my parents and my sister. My father was from Jamaica and he loved to play cricket. He was one of the star bowlers for the Windsor cricket team. Before the games, my father would warm up at home by doing his stretches and turns, then he'd dress in his cricket whites, do a few practice swings with his bat, and he'd be ready. The players also wore protective leg paddings because the cricket ball is very hard and could cause injury to a player's leg. What a pleasure it was to spend a beautiful summer's day with family and friends at the field. Families would spread their blankets on the sweet-smelling grass and we children would have fun running around playing our own games. I can remember when I was very young, trying to run onto the field to be with my father. I soon learned that this was a no-no. In my mind I can still hear the shout, "Bowl the ball, Burkey!" and see my father wind up and send the ball arching through the summer sky straight to the wicket. Cricket is a very long game and can take all day so they always stopped for "high tea." High tea was really dinner: rice and peas, coconut bread, codfish cakes, chicken, and so forth. My sister and I were always happy when we saw Daddy with a coconut because we knew he was planning to make coconut candy to take to the game. He was not a cook, but for some reason this was his specialty and it was delicious!

Sometimes my parents would leave us at home with my grandmother when the team traveled to New York, New Jersey, Rhode Island, Connecticut, and Canada. They also played visiting teams from England and Jamaica. Those were wonderful, happy days.

We also had a victory garden at Franklin Park and after work and especially on Saturdays, you could see the family groups walking up to the park to tend their gardens. They would have their rakes and hoes over their shoulders. Again, as far as I know no one ever stole anything; we'd just garden and enjoy each other's company. At the end of the season you'd have nice vegetables and you'd share with your neighbors.

On other weekends my mother would take me to places that she enjoyed and I too began a lifelong love of museums, concerts, and theater. We would walk to the Museum of Fine Arts or Mrs. Jack Gardener's Palace. She also took me to Symphony Hall and the Conservatory where I heard Marian Anderson, Roland Hayes, Mahalia Jackson, Paul Robeson, and others.

Saturdays were also a time for playing board games or cards or dolls. We'd have doll carriage parades and doll weddings. I liked to sew and design clothes and I can remember creating a tuxedo for the groom and wedding gowns for the bride dolls. When a doll lost an arm or leg or some other disaster occurred, we'd even have a doll funeral at which one friend could be counted upon to give a sermon. Saturday was also a great time for playing outside. There weren't many cars then and drivers really watched out for kids, so we played many games in the streets. We played dodge ball, ring-a-levio, kick the can, or we'd just mash down cans and go clomping around. There were so many other games that children played together: ten-twenty, hopscotch, double Dutch, one fast, territory, or mumbly-peg to name a few. We didn't have an abundance of bought toys. I did have a dollhouse and carriage and a pair of roller skates; every once in a while I'd lend one to a friend and we'd go skating around the street.

Relatives visited on Saturdays and after the adults had chatted with you for a while, you were to be seen but not heard. I would sit in the corner and try to listen in. Sometimes they would spell when they didn't want me to know what they were talking about. When they found out I was writing down the letters, they started to spell backwards. It took me a while to figure that out, but eventually I did!

There were many neighborhood movie houses when I was very young, and for twelve cents one could spend a Saturday afternoon at the movies. I often attended the Humboldt Theater that was right around the corner from my house. We were treated to a newsreel, cartoons, a western, and the feature film. Popcorn and some candy brought our total expenses for the afternoon to about twenty-five cents!

Sometimes, on special occasions when we went to downtown Boston, we would see the organ-grinder with his trained monkey. It was fun to give the monkey a coin as he was dressed up and would tip his hat in thanks.

I am really happy that I had an early life in Roxbury with my family. Looking back at many memories has been a wonderful visit to the past.

# THE SOUTH BOSTON PUBLIC LIBRARY AND ME

*Anna Irving*

WHEN I WAS attending classes at the New England Institute of Banking some years ago, I found the library an excellent place in which to do my homework. When I worked at home there were always interruptions by the doorbell, the phone, and of course there was always the temptation of the television as well. I found that math, English, psychology, as well as five programming languages took a lot of concentration. I was a working mother with five children. This kept me very busy.

Each fall the library has an art show, which is held in the lovely garden behind the library building. Many South Boston residents participate in this delightful show. Some of the art work is interesting as well as beautiful. We seem to have an abundance of talent in South Boston. Our local artists work in various mediums and have their own styles. The library serves refreshments at the show and a good time is had by all. Both my son, Tim, and I like to display our work. This past year I entered three studies of the Long Island Head Light. I had been on a day trip with the CIA (Castle Island Association) and was enthralled by this lovely, well-kept lighthouse. I painted it by sunlight, by moonlight, and in the new-fallen snow. Easels and tables have to be set up for the paintings and the overall preparation is a good deal of work, but the librarians seem to be untiring. They do in fact seem to really enjoy themselves. They serve punch and other refreshments as well. They are so full of energy and good will.

Each month the library also has a display of local artists which I always pause to admire. It is never boring. The librarians themselves are very artistic in the way they create eye-catching window displays that often reflect the holidays or the months.

There are frequent guest speakers sponsored by the South Boston Historical Society as well as the Friends of the Library. We have had talks on the building of the Cape Cod Canal, the evolution of the American flag, the horrible Coconut Grove fire, and Abigail Adams, as well as many historic subjects. Since South Boston was in the heart of the Revolution, there is always a great deal of interest in the history of our wonderful city and Fort Independence. President John Adams himself gave the fort its fitting name when he dedicated it. The warm-hearted and generous Friends bake many delicious cakes and cookies for these occasions. They serve coffee, tea, juice, and hot chocolate with the pastry.

I was for a short time the president of the Friends of the Library. It was part of my job to arrange for guest speakers and to schedule book sales. The books are donated by local readers and are always welcome. Book sales are of course a source of revenue to buy book racks and also to pay speakers' fees.

Each Thursday the library shows a movie. Usually on or close to Saint Patrick's Day they show *The Quiet Man* with John Wayne, which is a really great picture, especially if you are, like myself, of Irish extraction.

The South Boston Branch Library was the second branch library to open in the United States. It opened its doors in May of 1872 with only 4,360 books. It was located on the second floor of the Masonic Building on the corner of West Broadway and E Street. In 1948, due to the sale of the building and its close proximity to the City Point Library, it was voted to close the South Boston Branch, but the citizens protested and the library remained open. In June 1950 it moved to smaller quarters at 386–388 West Broadway where it remained until it was partially destroyed by fire on May 20, 1957.

The current library building was designed to be handicap-accessible. Its architecture is very modern with clean lines and many windows to ensure good lighting for the patrons of the library. The library has all of the most modern equipment and computers, which are used by all patrons old and young alike. The current structure is on the site of the old Lincoln School.

Reference: *BPL News*, vol. 23, no. 7, October 1972. Published by the Boston Public Library.

# ON HUBERT STREET

## *Marion Smith*

*These are Marion (Green) Smith's recollections of child-
hood in Roxbury during the 1930s and 40s, as told
to Virginia Busiek, Roscommon Extended Care Centers.*

MARION (GREEN) SMITH grew up on Hubert Street in Roxbury with her parents, Nathaniel and Portia, and her brother
Junior "Junie" for short. The Greens lived on the second floor
of an old-fashioned three-decker. On the first floor lived the Halliday
family. They had fifteen children. Marion's family was small enough so
that for years she and her brother each had their own bedroom. Downstairs the Halliday children lined up to sleep on the bed crosswise so that
the bed could hold more children. When one child turned on the bed, all
the children had to turn over together, and if a brother or a sister wet the
bed, well, you can guess what happened to all the rest.

You would think the Halliday children would have envied Marion and
Junie for having their own bedrooms, but it seemed that the opposite was
true. Marion could not wait to get downstairs to visit the Hallidays.

When the Halliday's electricity got turned off, they ate by candlelight. At
those times, Mrs. Halliday cooked in a big wok over a flame and the set

the wok in the middle of the table. The children each served themselves with a big spoon. Eating by candlelight! Sharing food from the big wok!

Marion begged her Mom and Dad, "Why can't we cook in a wok and eat by candlelight? When are we going to get the lights turned off?"

"Marion, don't you realize that the Hallidays are less fortunate than we are?" Portia Green would say to her daughter in frustration.

Marion begged her mother to cook "eat-and-shut-up" for the family.

"What is eat-and-shut-up?" her mother asked.

"Something delicious that Mrs. Halliday cooks." Marion and the Halliday children had mistaken Mrs. Halliday's remark for the name of the supper food. As Marion described it, Portia realized that Marion was talking about an especially cheesy macaroni and cheese dish made in lasagna pans so there was lots and lots of crust.

The Halliday children never got sick. Marion's brother got the mumps and later nearly died of diphtheria. Other kids got the chicken pox and measles. But the Hallidays were always well.

An Italian man came through the neighborhood selling every kind of fish from a pushcart. He knew the Hallidays and their fifteen children. At the end of the day, he bundled up all the scraps, fish heads, tails, fins, and spines and gave them to Mrs. Halliday. She pulled the fish meat from the bones and made a wonderful stew. Everyone in the neighborhood noticed the aroma. There must have been men asking their wives, as Marion had asked her mother, "Why can't we eat like the Hallidays?"

Mr. Halliday had a Tin Lizzie. On Saturdays in the summer he took his kids to Revere Beach with as many friends as could pile into the car. In the front seat sat Mrs. Halliday and three kids. The back seat held five or six more. Two or three more squeezed into the old-fashioned rumble seat. In our times, the police would stop a car loaded like that, but it was considered just another slice of life then. On the way to Revere Beach was a hill. The kids got out and pushed the old car. The car had no brakes. At the top of the hill, Mr. Halliday shouted to the kids to hop back in, and the car hurtled down the hill. Everyone held on for dear life. It was as good as the Revere Beach roller coaster.

Mary Robinson's family down the street had ten children. The Andrews family across the street had ten kids. The Hallidays had their fifteen. Everyone would go around together and people would say, "Here comes that Hubert Street Gang." Sometimes everyone went to the Franklin Park Zoo. One of those times, Tony Andrews fell into the bear pit. Some of the kids ran off to get the guards. The rest of us lay on the ground looking over the edge of the pit and begging God, "Please don't let Tony die."

Miraculously, Tony knew enough not to move or make a sound. He just lay on the ground and shook all over. The bear was in his den. He stepped into the pit, but did not see Tony. Three guards came. Two held in the bear with long pitchforks, and the other one lifted Tony out. When they got Tony out, they let him have it. They smacked him up the side of the head and hollered at him. You can bet our parents never heard a word about it until we were all sixteen and seventeen years old.

On summer nights on Hubert Street, there weren't electric fans or cooling devices. On weekend nights, the children were allowed to play on the sidewalk until midnight because it was so hot inside. It might be three o'clock in the morning before everyone would get to bed. We were perfectly safe because our parents were sitting on the stoops or leaning out the windows. At the end of the block the kids would be playing jacks. A few doors away they would be playing "aggies." At the next house, someone's father would be helping turn a jump rope for all the kids. My dad leaned out the window and sang, "Down by the old mill stream — not the river but the stream." He'd shout out, "All together now," and everyone would join in the song with him.

*Marion says that there could be people who might doubt that she's telling the truth. People that want to believe Roxbury-dwellers had a deprived life at best will not want to believe the richness of life in the neighborhoods. "Thank goodness Mary Robinson lives here at Ruggles, too. She'll back me up. She knows I'm telling the truth because she lived on Hubert Street, too."*

# Journeys

# I MARRIED IN
# TO SOUTH BOSTON

## *Mary Agnes Donovan*

I GREW UP IN MIAMI, having moved there from Georgia when I was just a toddler. My parents, Nell and Julian Harper, were dyed-in-the-wool southerners and did not care for Yankees. They had only two children—myself and my brother Harold, who was born when I was fourteen. My seventh grade civics teacher at Miami's Robert E. Lee Junior High School asked who could go to the board and write the word Massachusetts. I volunteered and spelled it correctly, little knowing that I would be living there in less than five years.

My husband and I met in downtown Miami on Labor Day weekend 1951, when he was on liberty from the Navy base in Key West. I was fifteen and he was nineteen. He was my first love and my first New England Yankee. He came from South Boston and intrigued me with stories of his escapades in Southie.

We eloped on January 21, 1953, the day Dwight D. Eisenhower was inaugurated as President of the United States. We married in Waycross, Georgia, and moved in with his parents and three sisters at 495 East Eighth Street in South Boston. He had a total of six sisters and one brother. The

house was six rooms on three floors, and the only bathroom was in the basement. It was a long trip to the bathroom in the middle of the night from the third floor bedroom!

My new in-laws were receptive of me, but my new sisters-in-law loved to tease me about my southern background. They called me "stupid rebel" and asked things like, did I wear shoes? I took it all in stride, but underneath, my feelings were hurt. I didn't think these were very nice things to say. I wasn't a stupid rebel — I knew I was smart. It was a putdown.

His family were all true Bostonians, and they observed the Saturday night tradition of franks and beans. Mrs. Donovan would sometimes make the baked beans from scratch, other times from a can. The traditional meal was Boston baked beans and brown bread, and the brown bread came from a can. I didn't like that brown bread. I don't think it's a tradition here anymore. We didn't have any kind of Saturday night ritual in Miami. The only southern tradition I remember was you were supposed to eat black-eyed peas on New Year's Day to bring you good luck.

I also learned about the New England boiled dinner, consisting of a smoked ham cooked in a huge pot with cabbage, potatoes, and carrots. Even an inexperienced cook like myself could be a success at this. A friend of mine told me, "If you can read, you can cook," so I got recipes from my mother-in-law (she had a big file with three-by-five index cards) or from magazines. I wrote to my mother frequently, asking for the family recipes like fried chicken, Toll House cookies, or duchess potatoes. My mother was an excellent cook. Mostly she sent me letters; I didn't have money to call her on the phone. In those days, long distance was expensive. I also followed directions on the boxes from the supermarket, like Spanish rice made with Minute Rice. I became a pretty good, creative cook.

In April, we started looking at ads in the neighborhood paper for an apartment. Some of the ads read "improvements," meaning they had continuous hot water. We did not have the money for such a luxury and chose a cold-water flat at 202 H Street, which intersected with East Eighth Street. It was a two-minute walk to the in-laws.

We moved in on May 1 and paid twenty-seven dollars a month for three rooms. Two of the rooms were good sized, but the third one was tiny, and we used it for a den. There was no tub or shower, just a toilet, and we had to take sponge baths or go to the in-laws for a tub bath. The floors were so slanted that a ball placed on one end of the room would roll quickly to the other side.

In September we moved to 498 East Eighth Street, right across the street from the Donovans. The apartment had two big rooms on the second floor, with a small room off the bedroom and a huge walk-in closet. The small room would be for the coming baby. The rent there was $5.10 a week, and the landlady, a white-haired, elderly woman, came each week to collect it. (I never figured out what the extra ten cents was for.)

This apartment had a tub and toilet, but the hot water faucet was not connected to the tub, so in order to take a bath, we had to carry many pots of hot water from the stove to the tub, which was just off the kitchen. There was a huge black iron stove in the kitchen that supplied heat for the three rooms. I cooked many meals on that stove, and there was always a full teakettle with hot water for the afternoon cup of tea. I used to peel an orange and put the peels on the hot stove, and the aroma would fill the entire apartment.

There were no clothes dryers in those days, but I was very fortunate to have a secondhand washing machine. Clothes were dried in the kitchen on a clothesline strung across the whole room. It usually held baby diapers, for there were no Pampers then. In the summer, I went to the roof, where my husband had put up a clothesline, to hang the laundry.

I have two fond memories of that apartment. One was September 21, 1953, when our first child, a daughter, was born. She was to be followed by four boys and three more girls over the next thirteen years. The second memory was September 1954 when my husband came home with a Singer sewing machine. It came in its own wood cabinet, and it was beautiful—a black, cast-iron head with gold lettering. With that sewing machine I made clothes for the children, even Easter coats. I was very happy whenever I was sewing. I still have it, and the machine works perfectly, only I had to replace the wood cabinet with a new one a few years ago.

While living at this apartment, my husband got a good-paying job at New England Portrait Service in downtown Boston at forty dollars a week. He had been a photographer in the Navy, and wanted to continue with this skill. That was an average pay in those days, but the money was still scarce. In 1953, World War II had only been over eight years, and the Korean War was going on. The country was still trying to get on its feet. There were no credit cards then, and vendors would knock door to door selling their wares. They usually had a catalog to look at, and you paid something down, and they would come around once a week to collect. I remember buying a Bible from a salesman for thirty dollars. It was very big and had places for recording the family births, baptisms, marriages, and deaths. I think they gave me a free pair of rosary beads, too, but that's still a lot of money for a Bible! It probably took me thirty weeks to pay it off. My husband was not very pleased, but I wanted it, and I still have it today, with the covers long gone. I can't bring myself to throw it away.

We also had a tab at the corner store, and they would let us run up to about twenty dollars. I would pay it up when I had the money, which was infrequently. One day I went to get some potatoes, which came to nine cents. I must have been over the limit, for the store clerk refused me. I was very embarrassed, and I never let it happen again.

What I liked most about Boston was its quaintness. The row houses, the gaslit lamps, and the ivy-covered homes. My favorite memory was the horse-drawn carts that used to draw me to the window when I heard "Rags! Rags!" It was the ragman, and you could sell your rags to him. There was even a horse stable at the corner of East First Street and H. I couldn't believe that there was a stable in the heart of the city, but my husband took me to see for myself. They finally tore it down in the sixties, and I felt sad to see it go.

I think I adjusted well when I first came to Boston. Most difficult were the cold weather and gloomy overcast skies. I was used to warmth and sunny skies. What I did like was the snow, and still do to this day. Although I wasn't born here, Boston has become *my* city. I love it here, and I would not live anywhere else.

# SAFE LANDING

## *Peg Foley*

I LIVED ON THE SAME STREET in the South End for fifty-four years, until I was forced to move because my building was taken over for taxes that were not paid. I came home from work one day and there was a big yellow sign on the front door informing the tenants that we would have to vacate the premises. I was in shock and devastated. I was born and brought up there and brought up my five kids there.

I formed a committee and fought to save the buildings for four years, meeting after meeting. We were successful but I still had to leave because I was not eligible for the subsidized rent that I had negotiated for the elderly. They were able to remain, their lives undisrupted. My rent, however, jumped from $100 to $595, so I decided to move to Southie. After a long search we found a nice apartment on East Third Street. It took me quite a while to adjust, but I survived and I'm very happy now. I've been lucky to have wonderful neighbors who made me feel at home in each of the three Southie neighborhoods we've lived in over the past twenty years, so it was a safe landing and I'm proud to say, "Southie is my hometown."

I worked at the Broadway Branch Library for five years where I met many wonderful people. I joined the "jet set" and took up line dancing and formed a network of ladies for friends. Dancing is a big part of my life now; it's great exercise and provides a wonderful social life. I am very active at the Senior Center at L Street. The best thing that has happened to me there is that I was taken under the wing of *Baska* (Polish for Barbara) and learned to knit and crochet. After driving Baska crazy I managed to make two afghans and several fun fur scarves, as well as a baby sweater set.

Besides the Senior Center, I also joined the Irish American Club and the CIA (Castle Island Association). With the CIA, I attend shows, go shopping, and take a lot of day trips. We also have an annual New Year's trip to the Three Points Hotel in Leominster. I go by the old adage, "Use it or lose it" so I try to keep active as much as possible. In fact, I am out of the house so much that my husband jokes about it. I am on the go all the time with my friends and if one of them calls the house my husband tells them, "She's out. You see her more than I do!"

My one traumatic experience was losing my forty-year-old daughter to lupus after a three-year illness. She was treated for rosacea at first and finally after several tests was diagnosed with lupus. My friends and neighbors were very supportive during this time. I realized then that Southie people really care and are the first ones to come to the aid of their own.

I find great peace at Castle Island where I do my walking and enjoy my Sully's hot dogs. One of my favorite pastimes is sitting on the benches by the statue with the boys, listening to their stories. They have me in stitches, and they don't even know they're funny. It's fun to hear the nicknames they've given each other: Edso, Micka, Peanuts, Ike, Meatball, Rabbit, Whacko, etc. They have a name for everything; they call the Old Colony "The Bricks." All the old-timers played football there on the various teams.

It's been a great time for me living here. My life now is peaceful and fun, the kids are doing great, and I'm enjoying my grandchildren and great-grandson. I'm eighty and hope to keep going in good health and keep a sharp memory. Remember, "Use it or lose it!"

# THE STORY MY MOTHER NEVER TOLD ME

*Sona Frissora*

RUMMAGING IN THE ATTIC one day, I came across a box of old crumpled newspapers and letters. These documents told the story I had never heard in full: that of the long journey my dear mother, Siranoosh Gulumian, made when she and her family immigrated to the United States from Turkey in 1922.

At merely seventeen years of age, she was detained at Ellis Island, separated from her family, and deported back to Turkey, all due to a technicality in immigration law. The Dillingham Law, as it was called, stated that "birth shall determine nationality." Although my mother arrived with her parents who were born in Armenia, she herself had been born in Constantinople, Turkey. At the time of their arrival, the Armenian quota was still open, but the Turkish quota had been exhausted and she was turned away. Further, her parents were detained with her for months for "accompanying an alien"!

My mother rarely spoke of this journey, but the New York and Boston newspapers reported the beautiful young woman's tragic story and made her a *cause célèbre*. They ran a winsome photograph of Siranoosh under

the headline, "She Pleads at the Gates of America." Due to the power of the press, she received many marriage proposals, both verbal and written.

My mother's brother, Nubar, was already a resident of Dorchester and had volunteered in the United States Army during World War I. In a special dispatch from the *Daily News* to the *Boston Globe* the headline ran: "Dorchester Veteran Fights for Admission of Relatives." The article went on to say that, "although he served in the [military] and is thus entitled to full rights of citizenship, Nubar Gulumian is called on to make the fight of his life to save his sister, father, and mother from deportation."

After going to federal court in New York, my uncle succeeded in having my grandparents admitted, but he was not able to save my mother from deportation — the Dillingham Law was the final word.

During the long months that she was detained at Ellis Island, the young Siranoosh learned to speak English as well as any American child and became a great favorite with the administration.

She helped in the kindergarten where she was befriended by a Mrs. Jennie Pratt, the director of the immigrant station school. Among the letters I found was one from Mrs. Pratt containing this touching remark: "Your stay at Ellis Island brought sunshine to many children's hearts as you were always ready to help them."

As popular as she was at the school, the next headline read: "Girl Deported as Writ Lands Parents." It is difficult for me to think of my mother, just a girl of seventeen, traveling thousands of miles alone. Although she stayed with relatives in Constantinople, I wonder what her feelings were when she had to leave her parents and brother, not knowing when the quota would reopen and she could see them again.

*Engagement photo of my brave mother Siranoosh Gulumian and my father Daniel Topjian.*

But return she would, and my uncle made sure she'd be able to afford the voyage when the time came: "Fare for Trip Back Follows Deported Girl." He saved up $202, the fare necessary for my mother to return to the United States. The quota opened up and back she came to America to rejoin her family, who had since settled in Dorchester.

Her name is now included on the American Immigration Wall of Honor at Ellis Island, along with thousands of other immigrants. I wonder what their stories are.

Although I knew that my mother had been deported, I knew none of the details until I found those clippings. How I wish my mother had told my sisters and me more of the story, especially how she felt through this scary ordeal. How good it would be if I could tell her how much I marvel at her courage and tenacity. I'd love to be able to give her a hug and ask, "Mom, how did you do it?"

I would hope that those reading this story will make sure their family has a "do ask, do tell" policy. Our stories are a rich part of each family's heritage.

# NAVY WIVES

## *Beatrice Jones*

I WAS BORN IN Allenton, Alabama to Henry and Anna E. McReynolds in 1931. I had one sister, Juanita, and two brothers, Walter and Dan. My dad worked at the sawmill, my mom cleaned the homes of white people while taking care of their children.

When I was six years old, my family moved to Pensacola, Florida. Everything in Pensacola was very different from Allenton; for the first time we experienced paved streets, fire trucks, running water, bathtubs, and a gas stove. We didn't know how to use anything! The move left a lasting impression on us kids.

When we started school, we were excited to see such large school buildings in comparison to the one-room schoolhouse in Allenton. All the schools were segregated. The white kids rode the buses while we walked the twelve long blocks to our school. Sometimes while we walked, the white kids would throw ink, spit on us, and call us niggers. We couldn't do anything but take it, and to make matters worse we received their old school books once they were finished with them. In our school, we were taught about Black History and learned the National Black Anthem.

When I graduated from high school in 1949, I tried finding work cleaning houses or babysitting. I walked through the neighborhood, knocking on

doors to get work and would often be greeted with "get away from my door, nigger." Words can not express how horrible this left me feeling. With my head held down, I would continue to the next door.

In 1950, I met my husband, Joseph Jones. He was in the Navy and stationed in Pensacola. We got married in 1952 and our first son, Joseph, Jr. was born. When Joe received orders to transfer to Mayport, Florida, I was happy to leave Pensacola but very sad to leave family and friends. After living in a segregated community off-base for two years, Joe got orders to transfer to Naples, Italy. Joe, Jr. and I moved back to Pensacola until the Navy arranged transportation and housing for us.

Seven months later, in 1957, we were told to take a train to New York City where we would be met by a Navy representative and taken to a hotel. Joe, Jr. and I were the only blacks there. I started to wonder what would happen next. The next day we boarded a luxury liner, the *S.S. Constitution*. There was happy music and everyone was laughing and happy. I stood on the top deck with Joe, Jr. thinking about home and cried. I was leaving all that I knew to go somewhere I didn't know. It left me not knowing what to think. A white Navy chief's wife asked me what was wrong and then put her arms around me. I started to feel better.

I really felt lost at first but all the military families got together and were introduced to one another. Joe, Jr. and I were still the only blacks. Nine days on that ship woke me up to a new day, and I began to show my real self. I felt like a new person. For the first time, I realized that I was just as good as white people.

Stopping in Spain, France, and the Riviera, we arrived in Italy and stayed for three years. It was like a new birth with blacks and whites going out, eating, dancing, picnicking, and attending church all together, something unheard of in the United States. I felt good. I was a part of a group that was not based on skin color. The military was like one big family. When our tour in Italy was over, we were sent to Newport, Rhode Island. Life continued to be happy and lots of fun. Three years later, we were transferred to Boston and lived in Columbia Point, which was integrated with civilians and military people.

Boston was a big transition for my family and me. We had never experienced such coldness in a community before. Blacks and whites hardly spoke to each other. Looking out the window one day, I saw a black sailor. I went down, introduced myself, and met his wife. Meeting them was a great turning point. I was happy meeting other military families. We all became great friends.

We joined Grant A.M.E. Church in Roxbury. Later, my daughter Anna Maria was born and then my son, Steven Douglas. My children grew up going to church and Sunday school every Sunday. Joe, Jr. graduated from Dorchester High School. When Anna and Steven started in the Metco* program, I was so happy. I was beginning to see some of the same things I saw down South and I didn't want them to experience that. You cannot avoid discrimination. I tried not to let them know what I had gone through. When busing started in Boston, all hell broke loose and I felt like I was right back in the South. White folks were really acting like they did down there. I think everyone was angry. I could feel it everywhere. I am proud my two younger children were in Metco. No regrets now about early morning rising and picking them up at dark. All three of my children went to college with no problems.

---

* "The Metco program was started in the 1960s to provide enhanced educational opportunities for urban minority students, to help integrate suburban school districts, and to reduce segregation in city schools." — Mass Dept of Education website (www.doe.mass.edu/metco)

In spite of all I experienced, I can say thanks to the Navy because it changed me from thinking that I was a nobody to making me feel that I am someone special. I have always told my children to hold their heads up high, walk with pride, and never look down. Today, I am proud of my experiences and what I have done as a result of them. I am proud to be a wife, a mother, and a grandmother. I am a woman of Pride.

# The Home Front

# A VIGNETTE IN THE
# LIFE OF A FAMILY

### "THE WAR IS OVER"

## *Anthony Frissora*

I F YOU KNEW MY FATHER, you could probably appreciate this story more. He and his bride, my mother, migrated here from Italy in the early 1900s. Although he had a deep pride in his Italian heritage, he was also a deeply patriotic American—to the point of being chauvinistic.

The first election cycle following his naturalization, he registered to vote. In the ensuing years, when women gained suffrage, my mother was known to be the first woman in town to cast a vote. This, in a town that was well-populated with long-standing "Yankee" families. Showing civic pride and responsibility, they voted together in *every* local, state, and federal primary and election, until the dictates of age and health problems decided otherwise.

Although my father never ran for public office, he believed in participation and was active in campaigns to support worthy candidates. This I enjoyed because it generally involved evening rallies when the men would gather several cars and we would drive all over the town blowing horns and holding flares out the windows and shouting for our candidates!

His pride in being American extended into our family life. At that time, in immigrant families, parents "traded languages" with their children. However, one day the family of a friend of my father moved into the neighborhood. They had about five or six children, some of them teenagers — and longtime residents — and not one of them could speak English. This so infuriated my father that from that time forward in our family, only English was spoken to and by the children. In his broken English, my father would say, "We are Americans." Such was his patriotism.

My parents conversed with each other in both languages. However, I was in the part of the family that did not get the benefit of learning a second language.

Concurrent with his deep pride in his Italian heritage, he was, as I have mentioned, a deeply patriotic American. He flew the flag on every holiday, and God help us if, when taking it down, we let it touch the floor. When I returned from the service and showed him how the flag is folded, well then, that became *de rigeur* — and, "Don'ta let ita toucha the floor!"

During World War II, two of my brothers and I, as well as an uncle (who was brought up by my parents) were in the service. Although my mother was apprehensive, my father felt a deep, quiet pride that we were serving America. In fact, an open pride.

One brother served with the Army engineers in the CBI theater (China-Burma-India); my other brother served with the Navy "Seabees" in Alaska; my uncle with the judge advocate general, in Europe; and I served with the Navy, in the "amphibs" on an LST (landing ship tank) in the Pacific.

I was the last one home, suffering the aggravation of the "point discharge system" having been changed just prior to my scheduled discharge. The Japanese surrendered on August 15, 1945, but I did not muster out until May of 1946. One night shortly after my return, there was a great family party. All of the immediate family and in-laws were gathered—about twenty of us.

Soon, the word was passed around for all of us to go down to the "canteen" in the cellar. The canteen was a room with concrete walls where my father stored his homemade wine. The wine was in barrels stored in a rack along one wall. On the opposite wall were shelves lined with home preserved fruits, sauces, piccalilli (green tomato relish), strings of sausages, etc. A single light bulb dimly lit the crowded room.

My father shushed us all for the "main event." In the far corner of the room, he had built, unbeknownst to me and my brothers, a concrete vault about two feet cubed. He had a sledgehammer and struck the first blow, and each of us—my brothers, uncle, and I—took turns in "unlocking" the vault. In it, buried in sand, was a small keg containing his wine.

My father tapped the keg and each of us had a water glass of a beautiful, clear ruby-colored wine. And there in the dim light, with the wine barrels, preserves, and sausages, and the joviality subdued to a murmur, we toasted our safe return. I looked up and there was my father wearing a look of pride and contentment, and my mother a look of relief, both with eyes slightly moist.

I thought to myself, *Yes, at last, the war is over.*

# MEMORIES OF
# PEARL HARBOR

## *Marion LeCain*

O N THE AFTERNOON of December 7, 1941, my friend Virginia Walsh and I were at the Regent Theatre in Arlington, Massachusetts, when the film was stopped and the manager came out on stage. "The Japanese have bombed Pearl Harbor," announced Mr. Flynn. "You should all go home — I'm closing the theatre." We sat in shock. Virginia knew that my father, Jim Mulloney, worked as a pipe fitter in the shipyard at Pearl Harbor and we were both shaken by the news. Both Virginia and I walked straight home. There were small groups of people talking in the streets. Virginia's mother asked me to stay at their house until my mother got out of work, but I wanted to be at home.

I prayed that my father would be alright. Had he been at work? Was he injured? Was he safe? It took several weeks to get the answers to these questions, weeks of sitting by the radio and listening to the news flashes. In the meantime, I tried my best to keep my younger brothers distracted with games and cards.

We had a telephone, but the news came to us in the form of an index card-sized piece of lined paper. *V-mail*, or victory mail, was the fastest way to contact or be contacted by anyone in the military. It was a letter written on a notepaper form that was photographed and reduced, which allowed censors to easily black out any sensitive information and which lessened the mail load. Father's letter said that he had been working that day on the base at Pearl Harbor and had been slightly injured, but was now okay and back at work. Father had a marvelous calmness about him even in the middle of chaos, but written into the corners of his letter were notes about the Japanese and cursing the attacks. After we finally received his letter and knew he was alright, I made a cake in his honor. The tension in the house eased a bit.

My mother had worked as a cashier before the war, but then went to work in the office at the Charlestown Navy Yard where she earned better pay and a pension. My older brother Jim decided to enlist in the Navy after graduation. I was fourteen and also had two younger brothers—Roger, thirteen, and Jacky, eight. Mother had relied on me for housekeeping, always, but after the U.S. entered the war I became chief cook and bottle washer for the family. With mother working and Jim gone, I was in charge of all the cooking, housekeeping, and looking after my younger brothers. I was a freshman in high school.

My brothers accepted the fact that I was in charge, and they did the jobs I assigned them, but I was the one cooking all the family meals and making sure they did their homework. Everyone at that time had blackout curtains, shortages, and rationing. There were coupon books for buying meat, dairy products, heating oil, shoes, sugar, and gasoline. Because of the rationing, shopping was a challenge. You couldn't say, "Let's have ham or meatloaf or a roast" because you couldn't know what would be available. We often had canned peas, green beans, or corn to go with our meal. I tried hard to have the traditional Saturday night dinners of baked beans and brown bread, but it was *catch as catch can*.

I have one vivid memory of the sound of trucks rumbling by our house in the dead of night transporting Army troops from Fort Devens to embarkation points in Boston Harbor. I remember praying for them as they passed by, but I never mentioned hearing them to anyone (*Loose lips sink ships!*).

There were war bond drives and many movie stars appeared for them; in fact, Clark Gable's wife Carol Lombard died in a plane crash while on a war bond tour. The money helped the war and kept people involved in the war effort as every little bit helped. There were also recreation places for the military called "Stage Door Canteens," but I was too young and too busy with school and caring for my family.

By May 1945, the war in Europe was over and in August 1945, the Pacific War also ended and our troops started returning. My father finally came home from Pearl Harbor and was transferred to the Charlestown Navy Yard. My older brother Jim came home with a southern bride who had been in the Women's Army Corps. My mother was not happy about that. Jim and his wife moved into the attic and you might say the war zone had come home!

# STORIES OF MY MISSPENT YOUTH

## *Joseph McHugh*

I WAS BORN in a three-decker at 219 West Third Street in South Boston in 1930. When I was four, we moved to East Sixth Street; then we moved to L Street; and finally to West Fifth Street, where my story begins at age eleven. I was the youngest of four children, with two older brothers, Jimmy and John, and a sister, Anna. My father worked as a longshoreman when he was well enough. We would later find out that he had Parkinson's disease. My mother ruled with a gentle hand and a slightly dampened dishtowel. I swear those dishtowels were an extension of a bullwhip. I would take a stinging hit even if I was only thinking something bad.

On a sunny Sunday afternoon I was given permission and twenty-five cents to attend a matinee at the local Broadway Theatre. The movie was suddenly stopped. The house lights came on and the manager announced from the stage that Japanese planes had attacked Pearl Harbor. I knew it was a big deal, but for the life of me I could not remember where Pearl Harbor was. The theatre emptied out and I headed home. There was a

complete change in the people on the street: everyone walked quickly; no one smiled. At the corner of F Street and Fourth, two old Irish men were talking about the big news. "We'll beat those little bastards in two weeks," I heard one say. They would have been much closer to the truth if they had said two hundred and two weeks.

Anyone who had access to a radio listened intently to the incoming news, and in the early months of the war it was all bad news. The Japanese were going through the South Pacific like gangbusters, and the German U-boats were creating havoc on our east coast. Because of the U-boats lurking off our coastline, our government adopted a strategy that was working well in England. In order to decrease the sky glow from the coastal cities, blackouts were introduced.

During the war, my mother, sister, sisters-in-law, and assorted female neighbors would get together and play cards on Saturday evenings. All the men were in the service, and my job was to go pick up hot, fresh donuts from the "Bakey" at Lark and Ninth streets. The blackout regulations required the gas streetlights to be painted black, thus making the streets very dark. If you didn't know the pitfalls in the brick sidewalk, it was easy to take a spill. Enter Mrs. Bourke's black watchdog. Most of the time the dog was penned up in the back of her variety store, but this night, as I gingerly wended my way to pick up the donuts, the black devil escaped and lunged at me out of the darkness. I fell stunned onto my backside and lay in a fetal position waiting for the next attack, but it never came; the black devil had run off. Uttering all the swear words a twelve-year-old was allowed, I picked up my ninety-five-pound frame and continued on to the Bakey.

SOUTH BOSTON

Between the ages of eleven and fifteen my time was spent babysitting, playing half-ball, being a pain in the neck, playing half-ball, helping in scrap drives for the war effort, playing half-ball, going to school to be reminded of my being such a dumbbell, and playing half-ball. Half-ball, for those deprived of the thrill, was played with a pimple ball cut in half with a razor blade stolen from your dad's razor. The bat was a broom handle found in the rubbish. The pitcher would stand on one sidewalk, the batter across the street. One early morning I was the batter. When I swung at a juicy offering from Tom Egan, the broom handle flew out of my hands in a looping motion until it smashed the front door glass of the house across the street. For a fleeting moment I thought of running from the scene, but I knew the owners would be knocking at my mom's door in minutes.

I needed money to fix the glass so I took a job at the Boys Club. When I finally made enough money to pay for the glass, my brother, who was home on leave, gave me a list of things to be picked up at the hardware store. I held the list tightly in my hand: putty, points, touch-up paint. Just as I was about to enter the hardware store, I heard, "Hey Red, do me a favor," from a rather seedy, down-on-his-luck kind of guy. I said, "Sure," and he handed me a dollar and asked me to get him a pint of denatured alcohol. I added this to my list and entered the store. Putty, points, paint, and a pint of alcohol appeared like magic. I paid, left the store, and met my new pal in the doorway next door. Just as I handed him the pint, I was pushed roughly aside by the store owner who had followed me outside. The pint was snatched from the grip of the poor man, and I received a swift kick in the backside for helping him buy a pint of alcohol. I knew nothing of his motive, never dreamed he was going to consume the colorless liquid. But I had a sore butt and my new pal lost the money he gave me, all because I couldn't hold on to a stupid broomstick and I broke a window.

In the early 1940s the government took by eminent domain a large swath of land in South Boston to build a housing development. Included in this land grab were many beautiful single homes as well as not-so-well-kept properties. Everyone was required to move. The government posted signs saying it was now their property, but the plans for the housing project were put on hold until after the war. These demolished homes became a prime source of firewood for the surrounding neighbors. With our homemade two-wheeled carts, we would go down Bowen Street to C Street and load up lumber for burning. There were other things of value to be "picked up." I will not use the word "stealing" because that would have to be confessed. Perhaps "purloined" would be a more genteel word. In those days all the plumbing pipes and stacks were sealed with oakum and a bead of lead. The lead, after being extracted from the pipe hub, could be sold to "Schneider the Raggie" for cash. Schneider drove a horse-drawn carriage up and down the streets and called out, "Rags, rags," to anyone who might want to trade. The adults in our neighborhood used to joke that Schneider could not work on Saturday because that was the day he was busy collecting rents on all the three-deckers he owned.

One day I was under a kitchen sink purloining the lead ring when I looked behind me and saw a pair of dress pants and shiny shoes. I had absolutely no way of escaping because my whole upper torso was wedged in the cupboard, so I slowly backed out from the cabinet and stood up to face the biggest, meanest government inspector in the world. He confiscated my trusty five-pound sledge, threatened me with much bodily harm, and threw me out the door. So on that particular day, Schneider the Raggie drove his horse and team down the streets of Southie with no benefit of trade from yours truly.

During the summer months just prior to the war, my friends and I went for long walks from our neighborhood haunts to the "mile road dump," a large area bordering South Boston and Dorchester used for dumping the refuse from the city of Boston. There, homeless men built shelters from wooden crates and cardboard. A half dozen of us urchins would go there on a Sunday afternoon to see the new huts and to throw rocks at rats.

During the war, the mile road dump became a prime spot for a prisoner of war complex called Camp McKay. The large numbers of Italian soldiers captured in North Africa in the early part of the war were sent to the newly opened camp. After Italy surrendered to the allies, these prisoners were considered non-belligerent captives. They wore the same uniforms as our GIs with a solid green shoulder patch to designate them as former POWs. They were still billeted at Camp McKay, but were free to associate with the Italian families living in the Boston area. The University of Massachusetts–Boston now rests on the sprawling area that was once Camp McKay.

During summer vacation my friend Jamie Connolly and I decided to seek work in a defense plant. Our plan took us from Southie to the tip of East Boston where there was a shipyard working around the clock. We both fibbed about our ages. During the war years, they would have hired a trained ape because help was at a premium. We were both hired to work the midnight shift. I was all enthused as I told my mother about my new job. She almost strangled me. There was no way her thirteen-year-old was going to be taking a street car to East Boston to work all night. Jamie's mom was of the same sentiment.

Shortly after our job quest, I joined a neighbor sitting on his front steps and told him about the job interview. He listened intently and said in almost a whisper, "Because you're dealing with the U.S. government, and the fact that you lied about your age in trying to get a defense job, the FBI will come to arrest you." I lived in abject fear of this for weeks. Finally I told my mother about my imminent arrest by the FBI. She said some very unkind things in Gaelic about this neighbor and told me to forget the whole incident.

～

The collection of newsprint from the neighborhood was a great help in the war effort and created a way for the kids to lend a hand. One Saturday I was stacking papers in the back of a truck with our new curate Father O'Leary. We were chatting and I thought it a good idea to invite Father O'Leary to my home for supper. He accepted my offer, and when I got home I told my mother that the priest was going to be our guest the following Wednesday night at six o'clock. I thought my mother was going to have a heart attack. One did not invite the parish priest to one's home on a whim. If there was someone close to death or I had been arrested, the priest would be welcomed. So much for being a nice kid.

The next Wednesday evening the kitchen table was set as if the Pope himself was coming. A sparkling, ironed white linen tablecloth covered the table, our best tableware was set with care, and my fidgety mother and I waited for the priest to arrive. Six o'clock came and went; six fifteen, six thirty, no Father O'Leary. My mother said he probably wouldn't come so she covered her prized linen tablecloth with the old *Boston Post* and we started to eat. Knock, knock, and in bounced Father O'Leary to a table covered with newspapers. The look on my mother's face was a combination of both horror and shame. The priest took no notice of the newspapers, enjoyed his food, and left. I wished I could have left with him — to say I was treading on eggshells for days after our dinner guest left is an understatement.

As the war continued and the casualties mounted, the sight of the Western Union telegram boys became a very common occurrence. Clad in dark green uniforms with visored caps, they were, for the most part, purveyors of bad news. Very, very few people owned a telephone during the war, so if the Defense Department had to notify a family of the capture, wounding, or death of a loved one, the onerous task fell to the Western Union boys. To see the bilious green bike parked at the curb, you knew something terrible had happened. I remember watching a bike rider come down West Fifth Street and stop outside the Hogan house. There were six Hogan boys in service and that day Mrs. Hogan learned that her son Jimmy had been killed.

On VJ-Day, I noticed a strange quietness in South Boston. Of course, people were very happy, as I was, but this fifteen-year-old just wanted my family together, my brother home, and to get back to some normalcy.

*World War II*
*ration book*

# Strong Women

# MEMOIRS OF
# HELEN McHUGH

## *Helen McHugh*

WHEN MY MOTHER'S DEATH came suddenly, I was overwhelmed with sadness, because you see I slept with her in the same bed. This didn't seem strange to me because nobody in my family of eight had their own room. We had to double up, and one of my brothers slept with my father. One night when I slept overnight at my girlfriend's house we decided to get up early, and as we passed her parents' room I was surprised to see her parents sleeping in the same bed. Confused, I questioned my girlfriend, and her response was "So what?" I couldn't wait to reveal all this to my mother. Her only reply when I told her was, "That's all right, dear." Still confused, I said, "Why don't you and Dad sleep together?" She told me to run along and mind my own business. My girlfriend was the one who had to explain things to me, and I was quite astonished.

Having my mother gone changed my life significantly. She passed away when I was sixteen, and she was waked at home. This was all very strange to me, having people come to the house at all hours of the day and night, paying their respects to my mother. I can still remember the big pur-

ple crepe wreath on the front door of my house. It bothered me to look at it.

I missed her terribly because she was always reassuring me how pretty I was, and telling me to stand up straight. Many nights I would come home from the school dance very discouraged because nobody danced with me. I always blamed it on my height, but my mother would put her arm around me and whisper things to cheer me up until I fell asleep.

My job after she passed away was to get breakfast and dinner every day for the eight of us. My father worked late at night. Just my younger brother and I were left in school, and he was two years younger. The others worked. Cooking became quite a chore for me, and I found myself calling my sister, Agnes, who worked at the gas company, just about every day to figure out how to make a meal. The stove had to be lit with a match, and I would light it and run because sometimes it would backfire on me. Mornings were the same thing, except my sisters and I took turns a week at a time. I dreaded that horrible alarm clock that would go off at six o'clock, and I wanted so much to roll over and ignore it, but I knew what would happen if I did that. A full breakfast had to be cooked every morning. Bacon and eggs, always. Lunches were made the night before, and it was nothing to put together more than a dozen sandwiches, dessert, and fruit. My brothers were treated like royalty. Come the summertime, I objected to these chores because all my friends were at the beach and I would have to leave early to prepare dinner. I also had to prepare my father's lunch on these days in the summertime, because he worked from noon until eight o'clock.

I never knew how he felt about losing my mother, and he never talked about her. You would never ask him how he felt, because you probably wouldn't get an answer. I could not get close to him or tell him how I was feeling. One day, a short while after my mother died, my friends were all going to the movies, and I asked him if he had twenty-five cents so I could go with them. He showed me all the change in his pockets and said he did have the money. I asked very politely, "May I have a quarter?" His answer was "Get your own money" — and he meant it.

At this point in my life, at the age of sixteen, I was old enough to get a job at Woolworth's, or as we called it, "The Fivie" or the "Five and Ten." I really enjoyed it. I still had to do all my other chores at home, and I didn't like that at all. I thought my sister was being mean to me. After all, I had a big job and I shouldn't have to do household chores, too. From the kitchen to Woolworth's, what a thrill. My boss's name was Ed Burgess and he was great to us. It was a large store; they sold everything from buttons to household items, and they had a candy counter almost as long as the store. I worked many counters, but my favorite was the candy counter. As I recall, a pound of nonpareils was about a dollar. There was also a large snack bar, and you could purchase a hot dog and a drink for under a dollar. My pay for the weekend was about twelve dollars, and I had to give half of this to Agnes for life insurance. That upset me quite a bit.

Agnes became my mentor and guardian. She was twelve years older than me, and she taught me how to sew and cook and have confidence in myself. She wanted desperately to send me to college but it was out of the question because we couldn't afford it. One Friday night after work I went to the school dance, and I dressed in one of Agnes's outfits. I thought I looked great but she never liked me to wear her clothes, so I sneaked out of the house to work. How she knew this I'll never know. I saw her coming down the aisle at work and I ran to the household department, where I threw an apron over myself and said "hello" as nicely as I could. The first thing out of her mouth was, "Do you have my clothes on?" I told her I didn't, but then she made me come out from behind the counter and I was caught red-handed. I never did that again, but her clothes were so beautiful and she made so many of them. She then started making dresses for me. I kept my position at Woolworth's through high school and one year of business school.

Life got a little easier for me, a sister got married, and the first thing I knew, I was out in the business world working a full-time job. I worked for an insurance company for about six months, and then asked my father if he could get me a job in the courthouse where he worked. His answer was, "Get your own job." Well, I did just that: I got a job at the telephone company as a clerk typist and, boy, was I proud of myself. I couldn't wait to tell my father about it. He couldn't wait to tell everyone he knew that his Helen "got a job at the phone company all by herself."

When I married and moved out of the city my father was very upset that we couldn't find something in South Boston. He was not a very demonstrative person and didn't quite know how to express himself. He was trying to say "Don't go," but didn't offer any sentiments at all. We told him that we were moving to Weymouth, and in his own little brogue he wanted to know if we would be near the town of "Sit-u-ate." The first time he came to visit us, he wanted to know who lived upstairs in our Cape Cod–style home. He thought it was a two-family dwelling. He came in to look at the house and couldn't believe his eyes when he saw that we had two bathrooms. He told everyone that his daughter had "two toilets." This, to him, was astonishing, as the eight of us grew up in a very small house without a formal bathroom. When the grandchildren arrived, my father would come to visit, eat dinner — and head straight back home. He never drove or owned a car, and whenever he was away from South Boston, he couldn't wait to go back home to the city.

My father passed away after my third child was born. My story ends by telling you I have three children, two married and one single, and I am the proud grandmother of two girls and three boys.

# STRONG WOMEN

## *Barbara Porter*

R ECENT NEWS STORIES about immigrant women who risk so much and work so hard to support their families caused me to think about a few of the strong, underprivileged, American-born women who, despite all odds, also make many sacrifices to bring about changes in their lives and the lives of their families. First and foremost, of course, is my mother.

Our family was not an emotionally expressive family, so I can never remember a time when my mother told me that she loved me. Nevertheless, when I reflect back through my childhood years I can see many ways that she demonstrated her love, not only for me, but for her entire family.

I was born and raised in Wellsville, Ohio, and, until my departure to Boston, had only ventured up to fifty miles away from home one or two times. Our family was close but poor, although we were blind to this fact since practically everyone else in the community was also poor. My parents divorced when I was about five or six years old. My mother, me, and my three siblings were then forced to move into my grandparents' three bedroom, ramshackle, sparsely furnished house. Oftentimes there were as many as twenty different people living at the house, including our grandparents, aunts, uncles, cousins, family friends, and hobos.

Our home was situated next to the railroad tracks so hobos would often jump off the train and stay with us anywhere from a few days to a few months. They stayed free of charge, and to my knowledge they never stole or committed any other criminal acts against us. They shared with us interesting stories about what was going on in the larger world.

Our small community consisted of less than ten thousand people. Since the town had only three grade schools and one high school, chances were very strong that you graduated from high school with the same classmates that you had started first grade with.

Our close-knit community was strong on traditions. For holidays such as the Fourth of July and Halloween, the village would go all out with weeklong celebrations and decorations. During summers we had the Italian festivals, carnivals, family-style picnics, swimming in the murky Ohio River or creeks, and small-town baseball rivalries.

The fall of the year would bring high school football and basketball games with their accompanying marching bands strutting down the main street of town, led by high-stepping drum majors and majorettes. After the band passed, the entire village would fall in behind it and accompany the band to the town field where the opposing team would be "roasted" at a large bonfire.

Then, during the late 1950s, our small secure world began to fall apart. The main industries in our section of the country were the china potteries and steel mills. These industries virtually supported not only our small village, but all the surrounding communities and businesses up and down the Ohio River.

Our area of the country had been experiencing a gradual decline in business for several years since the late forties and early fifties due to foreign imports of pottery goods and steel, but in the late fifties everything

came to a grinding halt. The steel mills and the potteries either closed or were forced back to a skeleton of what they had been in the past. Other businesses that depended on the mills and factories for support were also forced to close their doors. This included our one movie house, our fleet of one taxicab company, our cleaners, the bus line that formerly carried people to and from work, and our single large grocery store. Suddenly, people were without jobs and money.

Jobs in the potteries and good paying jobs in the mills had never been an option for black folks anyway, but the shutdown of those industries had an especially devastating impact on this population. Prior to the shut-downs, the only jobs available to minorities were jobs that no one else wanted, such as work as a domestic or hard, labor-intensive positions in the steel mills or iron foundries. Suddenly, secondary to the loss of indus-try, even these less-than-desirable jobs were taken over by others.

Neither of my parents graduated from high school but, fortunately, my mom was a tough, resourceful person. Following her divorce from my father, she supported her children as a single parent. She accomplished this difficult task in a number of ways. During World War II, when man-power was short due to the war, she worked outdoors year-round on the railroad tracks "tapping ties" until the men returned home from the war and reclaimed their jobs. She worked at times as a "bootlegger" selling il-legal liquor evenings and weekends, a domestic, a cook in our one hotel, and a barmaid in our local Elks Club. She did what she had to do when she had to do it to make sure that her children were fed, clothed, sheltered, and attending school.

Life became a little easier for our family once my siblings and I gradu-ated from high school and obtained jobs; my sisters and I as domestics and my brother in the steel mill. Eventually my youngest sister married an Army man and moved away; my older sister moved to another town;

and my brother, who hated the steel mill with a passion, joined the Marines. I married a recently discharged Marine in 1960 but remained living with my mother.

My husband worked as a seasonal worker picking apples for a while but due to lack of steady, decent-paying employement in the area, was eventually forced to join the Navy in order to support our family. He was later transferred to a naval ship in Rhode Island. We decided on my living in Boston because I had a cousin already living there and Rhode Island was only an hour's drive away. Up until this time most of what I knew of Boston and other large cities was what I had read about in my seventh grade history books.

Magnolia Street in Roxbury was my first introduction to Boston, and what an experience! There were row upon row of huge brick three-decker houses lining each side of the street. The houses appeared to be jammed up against one another and there were no yards or grass. Women were sitting on the stoops and children playing on the sidewalks and in the streets, neighbors arguing, loud music playing against blaring police sirens all day and all night, and flashy cars racing up and down the streets. Everything was new, strange, busy, and noisy. Nothing like anything I had ever been exposed to in Wellsville.

The first obstacle I encountered after arriving in Boston was the language. Everyone spoke in what I first thought to be an unintelligible, fast, foreign dialect. I was constantly having to ask, Huh? Huh? Understanding the Bostonian lingo took a lot of getting used to. I have to admit though, that Bostonians in turn had just as hard a time understanding my hillbilly/southern/country drawl.

The Orange Line train was my next obstacle. It was on the Orange Line that I experienced my first ride on an elevated trolley, and I'll carry that experience with me to my grave. My first glimpse of the elevated train was not very confidence-inspiring, but after boarding the slow, wobbly, creaking, moaning, and groaning train and approaching Dudley Station, the little confidence I had took a sudden nose-dive. Suddenly, halfway into the curve the train jerked and slowed down even more, and then it started to tilt almost totally on its side. On peering out the window I saw the sidewalk rushing up toward me. I thought the train had fallen from the tracks! I gripped my seat tightly and gave out a scream that startled and amused everyone on the train.

Via the classifieds in the *Boston Globe* I found a job my first week in Boston at an electronic factory in Needham. My wages were a hundred dollars per week and I felt as though I had hit the lottery! At home it would have taken me at least five weeks to earn that much! And the work was easy. At home, after a day of backbreaking labor I would be bone-weary, physically and emotionally drained, and barely able to climb into bed at the end of a work day.

On a more positive side, I encountered a number of "firsts" in Boston. For the very first time I saw black firemen, policemen, social workers, nurses, doctors, and college students. Over time I began to wonder about what I had been doing (or not doing) for the past twenty-seven years of my life, since most of these people, like me, did not necessarily come from affluent backgrounds.

After a few years the initial glow around the way my life was playing out began to fade, and I became dissatisfied with the repetitive nature of the work I was doing. I realized that I had to work to survive in Boston, but I thought that the least I could do for myself and my family was to work at something that I enjoyed doing. But a career choice and the money to finance the choice remained a dilemma.

Then things began to fall into place for me. In 1965 the *Bay State Banner* newspaper came into existence and offered information around many educational and job opportunities specifically for minorities! It was through the *Banner* that I learned of Roxbury Community College (when it was located in Grove Hall), the federal Model Cities Program, and the Action for Boston Community Development (ABCD) program, which all offered many free or low-cost educational opportunities including remedial education assistance.

I graduated from Wellsville High School in 1954 but had not invested too much effort into my schooling since I had no higher educational aspirations at that time. Once in Boston I went through many starts and stops in my first few attempts to further my education. My first serious attempt took place in the mid-sixties. While continuing to work full-time at a factory, I enrolled in and completed an evening remedial education program sponsored by the City of Boston. Following completion of that program I enrolled as a part-time student at Roxbury Community College. Trying to get through the math and chemistry with my limited educational background, plus working full-time and balancing care of a family was very stressful and proved to be more than I could handle, so eventually I withdrew from school.

I continued to work at the factory but still held on to my dreams for something better. By 1969 my extended family, which included my mom (who had traveled to Boston with me), my two sisters and their families, and my brother, had joined me here in Boston.

My older sister eventually enrolled in the Boston Trade School Practical Nursing Program (LPN) and invited me to her graduation. It was as I witnessed her candlelight graduation ceremony—a sea of white uniformed students gliding down the middle aisle of a dim auditorium carrying lighted candles, with soft inspirational music playing in the background—that I decided I was going to be a nurse.

I went on to graduate from the Boston City Hospital School of Practical Nursing (LPN) in 1971. Once again it proved to be a difficult balancing act between school, job, and family life, but I was able to accomplish this goal with the assistance of my mother who, though she worked full-time evenings in housekeeping at BCH (*her dream job*), had always been there for me with the care of my children. She willingly and unhesitatingly assumed more responsibility for my children during this period of time, such as visiting their schools, monitoring their homework, and allowing me free time to study. Were it not for the sacrifices my mom made for me, I know that I would not have been able to complete my studies.

Immediately upon graduation from the LPN school I was hired by BCH as a staff nurse. I loved my job there and very seldom missed work unless it was a real emergency. My coworkers were great, the doctors were great, and even the patients were great. Most of the people that I first met there remain my close friends today. Working there was like being embraced by a warm, loving family.

My decision to return to school in the early 1980s, like other life-changing events in my past, was not very well thought-out. Although I was now working in my dream career as an LPN, once again I was beginning to suffer some discontentment around nursing limitations that are placed on LPN positions. This was my motivating factor for becoming a Registered Nurse (RN).

And so, with the emotional and financial support of family, friends, and BCH, I enrolled in a program that was offering an "easy" LPN-to-RN transitional program. I realized during the first semester of the program that I was in over my head academically. But I also realized that I couldn't just walk away this time because I had too much money and other people's faith invested in the project. Two things saved me.

The first was that the nursing program came with all sorts of built-in, free mini-workshops for students like me who required extra assistance, including study techniques, test-taking skills, and math and science reviews.

The second thing that saved me was my fellow LPNs who were also enrolled in the transitional nursing program. These were strong women who were older and fewer in number than the average students in the traditional nursing program. We came from all walks of life, but we were a

*Wellsville, Ohio, 1943*
*"The good old days."*

cohesive, supportive, and committed group of people. We were all working full-time jobs in hospitals or clinics and working hard under nerve-fraying daily routines of trying to balance family responsibilities, jobs, schools, and mates. We were chasing the dream hard.

One student was a single mother of an adolescent, as well as the co-owner of a start-up business. Another student was happily married, no children, and co-owner of a thriving business with her husband. Then her husband, without warning, walked out on her during the middle of the program. She was crushed but carried on. There was also the Latina immigrant from Central America who was helping to support a husband and children. She became pregnant near the end of the program but still managed to graduate along with us. Another student, whose mother died out of state and was buried on a Friday, was in class, seated for her finals that Monday. When the exam was over, we were waiting outside the door for her. She looked limp as a dishrag and said she found it hard to concentrate. Nevertheless, she passed the final.

This program was extraordinarily stressful and demanding. The incidents above are but a few of the personal issues that our small group was experiencing that came to mind whenever I started to feel sorry for myself or was having a bad day. Fortunately, at some point during the day or week we would all come together if just for a few minutes, to offer support, comfort, and sometimes humor to one another throughout the entire five years that it took us to complete the nursing program. Following graduation, we all went our separate ways and I have not been in contact with any of them since. But I will be forever grateful to them for the love and support I received when I needed it most.

My mom passed away several years ago, but she lives on in my heart. Though she did not have an opportunity to witness my graduation from the Registered Nurse program, I will be forever grateful to her for her legacy of unselfish love, commitment, and work ethic that she instilled in me.

And I cannot forget Boston. Boston has been very good to me and my family. Boston has opened up a whole new world for me.

# UNCHARTED WATERS

## *Barbara Signor*

ONE OF THE REASONS I accepted a job in Washington, D.C., is that I did not want to work at my father's bakery anymore. My father and uncle were partners at a retail bakery that made cupcakes, pies, apple and raspberry turnovers, fig, apple, and lemon squares, éclairs, coffee rolls, and that sort of thing. Drivers would order things, and we made and filled the orders.

I knew I wanted to do something else, but in reality I did not know what I wanted to do. I graduated in June 1951 from Girls Trade High School in Boston, and the summer of my graduation I worked at Camp Taka-hontay in Gloucester, Massachusetts, as an assistant cook. But I just knew that if I returned to South Boston in the fall, I'd be working at the bakery, eventually my brother would be in charge of the family business, and that would be the rest of my life, right there.

My friend Janet had gone to Washington in our senior year at school. She had an aunt who was a cook for Joseph Grew, the former ambassador to Japan. The family wanted a maid, and Janet's aunt suggested her niece for the job. Janet was the one who recommended me to the family that employed me.

I had never met my employer and was employed sight unseen. She only knew me from our phone interview. When she told me that I would be paid one hundred dollars every month and would get paid every two weeks, I accepted. I would have my own room and bath. I would have two half-days off on Thursdays and Sundays. My new employer told me that she would be wearing a gold or yellow riding cap when we met. I told her that I would be wearing a light blue dress with a black belt and large black buttons.

I took the train from South Station. This was my first time on a train, and the first time I had traveled so far from home. And when I arrived in Washington, I began to see the world in a very different way because I was on my own and I had entered a different way of living.

At that time, Harry Truman was the President. He lived at Blair House, across the street from the White House, because the White House itself was being remodeled. Dean Acheson was the Secretary of State, and my employer's husband worked for him.

The area that I lived in was quaint: the sidewalks were red brick, and most of the houses had black steel fences. The house had three stories — the first had a wide hall with a table near the door for the mail, and three big rooms. The front room had shelves on the left wall, from the floor to the ceiling, filled with books, with a window separating the shelves. The second floor had two bedrooms. The master bedroom and the guest room were there, along with a full bathroom. The third floor had one full bath and two bedrooms for the two daughters; the older girl was away at Milton Academy, back in Massachusetts. The younger girl lived at home and went to school in D.C. I also used to sit for her, as the parents had to go out a few times a week.

My room was at the foot of the stairs in the basement. It was small, with just a chair and a bureau and closet, but it had a full bath. There was a window in my bedroom, and I used to smoke so I always had my window up. I was supposed to work for the family from September until June, but when they asked me to go with them to New Hampshire for the summer, I refused. They had always been very good to me, but I didn't want to be a servant in their house forever; I knew that life just wasn't for me. Even when I lived in their house, I refused to sweep the front steps. It was the only task I ever refused to do, and I refused to do it because the bus stop was at the front of the house and I didn't want anyone seeing me.

I had at one time thought it would be nice to join the FBI, but when I wrote and asked about the qualifications I discovered that you had to have gone to college and that in most cases it would be helpful if you were a lawyer or had knowledge about the law. I knew that this was not for me. But while I was in Washington I had gone to an Army recruiter to sign up for the Army. This was when I found out that although I was eighteen years of age, I still had to have my father's signature.

I decided to join the Marine Corps because I wanted to escape. To go into the service was a legitimate way to leave home. You learned a trade, you got free meals, and you got paid. So I went to the courthouse on Milk Street and took my Armed Forces Qualification Test and passed, and then I was sworn in. I was to learn in two days that I needed to go to Parris Island.

The sergeant gave me a paper for my father to sign, but I asked for another one because my father sometimes made mistakes when he wrote. He gave me the extra paper. I, of course, signed one in advance because I was not sure that my father would sign the one that I gave him. I told him the day before I left that I was going away because I had joined the Marines. He knew that he had to sign a paper, and when I told him that I had already signed his name on one of the papers, he did sign the other one, which I turned in to the sergeant at South Station. No one saw me out of Boston.

Here I was again, going away from Boston. I was again on my own, making my own decisions. I was going to be in the Marines for four years, and I was heading for boot camp. World War II was over. There was a war going on in Korea, but at the time it wasn't being called a war—it was a conflict.

All I can remember of my first day at Parris Island was waiting in line. And it seemed a long wait. We had to tell our name and our serial number. Somehow I did manage to memorize it, and to this day I can rattle it off quicker than my Social Security number. The following day we had to see a psychologist. His question for me was did I think I could go through boot camp. My answer to him was if you had a father like mine, boot camp would be a cinch. After boot camp I went home for a few days before I went to North Carolina. I saw old friends but in my heart I knew I had made the right choice in going away.

But when I left for Cherry Point after my short leave I discovered a different aspect of the United States. I left Boston by bus, and when I got off to transfer for the bus to Cherry Point, I went into the waiting room with my luggage.

I had gone to school with colored girls at the Trade School. This was the term we used for African American individuals. I did not recall ever reading or being told that colored people down South were treated differently than up North.

I was sitting in the waiting room when an elderly gentleman told me I could not sit here, as it was for the colored folk. He pointed out the area I was to sit in, and then I saw the signs. White only. Colored only. I was red in the face. I was embarrassed, and felt so uncomfortable. I could not believe what I had seen on those signs. I did move into the whites-only waiting room, and as I recall I was the only one there.

When the bus came, I again went through another humiliating experience. Maybe "humiliating" is the wrong word to use. I automatically went to the back of the bus, as there was a free space there. I sat down and was told I could not sit there, as it was for colored only. At home my friends and I always sat in the back of the bus, as you could have more fun there. I had to sit in the middle of the front of the bus. Again I had to move. This was in the 1950s, and the girls, African American young girls who were stationed at Cherry Point, off-base, were treated as second-class citizens.

Looking back at that time in my life I think it took a little bit of courage to do what I did. Girls did not leave home, unless they were going to nursing school or college or the convent. I was stepping into uncharted waters. It was a bit scary, yet at the time it was adventurous. Living down South for a few years was a big eye-opener for me as to how we in America treated people. This was America, but an America I did not feel comfortable being in at that time.

# Vocations

# THE LIFE OF
# AN INTERPRETER

## *Mary Frasca*

I WAS ALWAYS a little interpreter. Italian was my first language but I learned English quickly. In first or second grade, my teacher told me to ask my mother for two dollars to buy an English primer. My mother thought I had misunderstood, because how could I read an entire book in English? Our upstairs neighbor checked with the teacher who confirmed the request, confident in my learning abilities. Of course, my mother gave me the money and soon I learned enough English to be able to read the book.

I went to the library every day to pick up books in Italian for my father and in English for myself. I loved to read. I remember falling asleep in front of the stove, a book in my lap and my feet propped up on the oven door for warmth. Some of my favorite books were *Penny Goes to School*, *Penny Grows Up*, and *Penny Gets Married*.

My interpreting began mostly for my mother. My father had a shop on Broad Street, making women's shoes, so he had to speak English to run his store. I was the bookkeeper, though. I remember at seven or eight keeping my father's books: I would first put the income then deduct the expenses and tell him the net income. I believe that is why I am good at math today.

My mother spoke mainly Italian and some broken English. She didn't have to learn English to do her shopping because the North End merchants knew Italian. She did need me to translate for doctor's appointments, though. That skill followed me throughout my life and career.

In school, I studied classical Italian. This differed from the dialects most people spoke, and was used in publications and on radio and TV. Now students in Italy study this pure form of the language, but in my parents' time, school was not mandatory in Italy, so many people could not read or write. I loved it so much and was good at it, so I was called upon to write letters to relatives in Italy, for my mother and neighbors. After I graduated from college, a neighbor told me about a job opening at an Italian newspaper, the *Gazetta del Massachusetts* (now the *Post-Gazette*). I worked there for twenty years, and also at the Continental Insurance Company in the legal department, and at the North End Union as a secretary.

I'm proud of what I do. My love for the Italian language is so deep I can't explain it; maybe it's because it was my first language. The language itself is beautiful, so melodious. And I get a huge satisfaction from helping people. For example, there was a woman in our community who spoke the Calabrese dialect. Because this is such a difficult dialect to understand unless you are from that region, sometimes people hesitated to try speaking with her. It wasn't that people didn't like her, they just couldn't understand her. So often she sat alone. But I like to listen to people talk, even if I can't understand every word. She clearly enjoyed conversing, so I visited her whenever I could and asked her questions about her family, grandchildren, etc. One day I missed a visit, and the next time I visited her, she told me how much she enjoyed our conversations. *"Quando*

*tu vieni, mi schiala.* ("When you come, I enjoy myself.") That made it all worth it.

Being an interpreter has its touchy moments, too. One of the hardest things I had to do (I was in my early twenties) was read a letter to my parents from my brother who was an infantry soldier in France. I had to tell my parents that my brother was wounded, and that his buddy from home had been killed beside him in the foxhole. This was a couple of days after D-Day. My mother nearly went out of her mind. But I knew I had to translate every word and not cover it up. I could not hold back; my parents had to know the truth.

Another touchy experience showed me the importance of interpreting in medical situations. I was about thirty, and my mother was sick and in the hospital at Mass General. She had chills and fever and needed another blanket. At home, when we ran out of blankets, we'd spread our coats over the bed to add another layer of warmth. So in the hospital, she asked for her coat. Thinking that she was going to get dressed and leave, they tied her down. They called me and when I got to the hospital, she was crying. I said, "Mom, what did you do?" "I didn't do a thing. I just asked for my coat." She was so embarrassed at being tied down, she was in tears. From that day on, I said, "I'm going to be an interpreter."

And that's what I did. I worked at the City Hospital (now the Boston Medical Center), and the New England Medical Center, interpreting. I also worked at the Greater Boston Elderly Legal Services as a paralegal, and a lot of committees at city hall, all of which involve some interpreting.

I get a lot of satisfaction from letting people express their views. Especially in medical situations, I must translate very precisely because patients need to understand accurately what is going on. Also, I keep their information in confidence. Once at the New England Medical Center,

I didn't want to interpret for a man because he was a neighbor. But he insisted, so I did. Later, his sister asked me, "What did my brother tell you?" I said, "Go ask your brother."

The first translating job I was paid for was one of the most fearful moments of my life. The patient was a woman on dialysis with whom I'd been working for several weeks. She spoke Italian and Spanish, having been born in Italy and lived in Venezuela before coming to America. She needed a kidney, and her daughter was willing to give her one. The woman and her daughter spoke Spanish to each other (which I couldn't understand), and the daughter understood only a little Italian and English, while the doctor spoke only English. With all these languages flying around, I had to be very careful. In the end, the mother decided she'd rather die than take a kidney from her daughter.

My sons have also picked up the language gene. One of them speaks nine languages and teaches Tamil, an Indian language, at Harvard.

One funny moment happened when I was translating for a couple of men from the Italian Cabinet who were visiting Boston from Rome. A representative from the consulate had brought them to the New England Medical Center for eye treatment, and the hospital called on me to translate. As they were leaving, they needed directions back to their hotel. Too embarrassed to tell these distinguished men they were in the "red light" district, I translated "combat zone" literally: *zona di combattimento*. For a moment, they looked horrified. "People are going to shoot at us?" Then I explained where they were, and we all had a good laugh.

# BECOMING A BARBER

*Mattie Powell*

MY HUSBAND WAS a barber and the owner of three barber shops: the Hollywood, the Powell, and the Star. The Hollywood was located in the South End at Worchester and Tremont Street. The Powell Barber Shop was located on Blue Hill Avenue between Quincy and Holburn Street. We purchased it from a man named John Reid. It was the first black barber shop in Roxbury. The Star Barber Shop was located at Grove Hall at the corner of Blue Hill Avenue and Washington Street.

I kept the books for all three shops. Each had three barbers employed. One day while walking by the shop on Blue Hill Avenue, I noticed that the shop was crowded with customers. The next day I observed the same activity. Yet this shop was always taking in the lowest amount of money. In that day one had to rely on the honesty of the employees: there was no means of counting the customers unless rung up in the cash register. I was desperate trying to decide what to do when I was certain I was needed in the Powell Barber Shop, because that one in particular always came up short and I thought my presence would make a difference. It was then that I wanted to become a barber.

First, I had to go to barber school. I discussed the idea with my husband and he reluctantly agreed. He said, "Don't forget you will be the only woman in the shop." I was sure I could do well, but I was afraid of the razor. I had watched my husband skillfully using his razor to give a shave. The haircuts were cool; if only I could muster up the courage to conquer my worst fear. However, I was certain that practicing would free me from the tremendous fear. I entered a barber school that lasted for six months. My clippers, combs, clipper blades, shears, and my razor (carefully placed in its case) were arranged in my barber bag along with the barber textbook, notebook, and pens. So I was on my way.

I was happy to find that another lady had registered. We knew each other before so she was able to help me with studying the book, memorizing ligaments, nerves, and muscles of the body to prepare for the first test. (At first, I wondered what all of this had to do with the head, but I learned that the scalp massage we gave affected the rest of the body's circulation.) The instructor called my name and assigned me to a barber chair and stand. I placed the tools in the sterilization liquid. A big hair cloth was given to cover the customer to keep him free from the falling hair. A paper towel was placed around the neck and I was ready for my first haircut. "Next!" I boldly called.

The instructor showed me the different blades for cutting the hair in different lengths. I began at the back and worked my way to the crown of the head. "Not bad at all," the instructor said. Then he smiled and whispered, "The young man wants to get a shave, also."

I felt faint as I pictured the white lather turning red before my eyes. I spent some time trying to soften the stiff hair with hot towels and plenty of shaving cream. At last, I reluctantly picked up the razor and began to do the fourteen strokes it took to complete the shave. My instructor was watching me as he was aware of my fear of the razor. He approached the chair and said, "Mattie, all you can do is cut him."

Why did he have to mention the word "cut"? That was my fear, that I may cut someone. To my relief, the lather remained as white as snow. I was happy to place a hot towel over the face and not see a trace of red. The shave was complete. I graduated passing the book examination along with a beautiful haircut and shave as a demonstration.

My next appointment was in the Powell Barber Shop. I went to work in my white starched barber coat. Soon I noticed I had a problem. No one wanted to sit in my chair. They would say, "Thank you, but I will wait." Then they would get in one of the other chairs in the shop. Of course, these were experienced barbers of many years. It was heartbreaking to be rejected, but I watched my coworkers and learned a lot by just watching. I tried to be pleasant enough, but a woman barber was just strange to them.

Then the idea occurred to me to cut the kids' hair, so while the fathers were getting their hair cut, I cut the little boys'. I did my best to make it look as professional as possible. I was constantly being watched. Finally a man would give me a chance. Another would see he came out alive so then he would get in my chair. Before long, I had fathers as well as their sons. My business grew to include little boys, teenage young men, and adults young and old. Even ministers frequented the shop; they said they liked the atmosphere—no swearing, smoking, or loitering. I worked for eight years in that shop and became a master barber. The community had broken the discrimination against the woman barber. We could cut hair and give shampoos, massages, and shaves as good as the men.

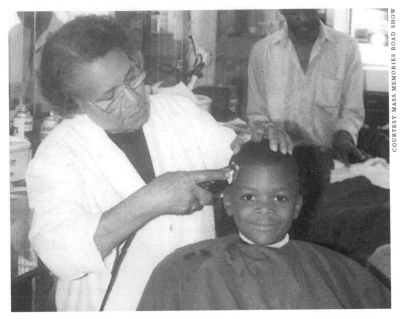

*Mattie and customer. "I always liked working with the children."*

The style of haircut changed in the eighties to the almighty Afro. Everyone wanted to be in style. That was bad for business because customers only needed a trim about every three weeks. It was this style that put an end to my career as a barber except on Saturdays when I helped my husband in his shop.

I went back to college and obtained a master's degree in early childhood education and worked in the Boston public school system for twenty-three years. I am now retired, with an active social life, but to this day I still renew my barber's license.

# ARTIST

## *Eileen Richardson*

I WAS BORN IN BOSTON in 1943 and brought up in Roxbury. My mother was born in Ireland on November 8, 1909, and my father in 1894, in Gloucester, Massachusetts. He was born on *his* father's birthday, October 8, and then *I* was born on *his* birthday, all on the eighth! My grandmother, my father's mother, belonged to the Red Man Club and Grange and was part American Indian. Dad was a patrolman with the Army when I was born and we had ancestors in the Civil War and the Spanish-American War.

I was thirty-seven years old when I moved to South Boston in 1981. I was happy to get my apartment in the Old Colony project. There were only four apartments in the building, and I finally felt safe after living in some horrible places. I could go out at night and walk around and talk to the neighbors who sat outside. I had a big apartment on the first floor on the main street. The bus went by it, and I had a garden with two forsythia bushes planted out front. Kids tried to pull them up, and then one day a woman ran into one bush because she'd lost control of her car and couldn't stop. That was the end of that bush! I had a Chihuahua, Juliet, and my cat, Garbage Belly, to keep me company. I helped stray cats at the Old Colony project, and then Donna Bishop would take the cats and spay

them and find them homes. I eventually won an award from the Alliance for Animals, and received it at a special dinner.

For me, one of the most important things about South Boston was the community of artists I found when I moved to the neighborhood. At one point, I was going to painting classes four times a week: Tuesday and Thursday, I had class at Condon; Wednesday's class was at Laboure; and Fridays I spent at the Curley Recreational Center. Sometimes I traveled over ice and snow to get the chance to paint.

I'd always liked painting, and I guess you could say I inherited some talent from my father and grandfather. My father won an award for penmanship once, and my grandfather was good at drawing, so we had a lot in common that way. As a teenager, I used to paint by myself. I drew a picture of a flower in Saint Joseph School, and my teacher loved it and asked the nun if she could have it. I only painted on white cardboard back then, which was hard; I didn't know anything about painting on canvas until I moved to South Boston.

After I moved there, I read in the *South Boston Tribune* about some free art classes at the Laboure Center, and I signed up. The class was held at an old apartment in the D Street project, on the first floor. It had old sinks and an old kitchen, where we would all have coffee on our break. Sister Adelle Waters, an oldish nun from the South, was our teacher, and there were about six students, including two plainclothes nuns.

I went to this class on Wednesday nights, until it was shut down. I climbed over snow banks to get to class, and I carried my supplies on my luggage carrier. I painted in oils and acrylics. I was a really fast painter, a free painter.

One day, a man, another student, came to my class and looked at the painting I was working on, which was a ghetto scene. He said that he wanted to throw the painting out the window, and that "No one will buy that. It looks like Roxbury." (It *was* Roxbury!) Well, he *did* throw it out the window, and then he left the class and never came back. The teacher went outside and got it back for me. Later, I sold that painting.

I liked painting so much that when I learned about other classes, I signed up for them. For instance, I found out about Marie Ugo's class on Friday afternoons at the Curley Recreational Center, also known as the L Street Bathhouse, on the beach. It was a big room, where the elderly have lunch and the Castle Island Association meets in the winter. Marie Ugo's sister-in-law would drive Marie and me to art class. There were two other girls in the class.

Marie Ugo was good to us. She was a Marine during the war and she was very organized and encouraged us to work hard. She volunteered her time to teach us and got us a show at the Shawmut Bank window and helped us when someone wanted to buy a painting. She said, "Get these paintings framed. I want them in the Shawmut Bank window by Monday morning!" And we made sure they got framed. I did two boat paintings in her class and exhibited them in the window. A visiting Irishman walking by the bank wanted to buy both of them. Marie handled the sale for me.

I exhibited with Marie in the South Boston Library, and I was so proud to exhibit with her. We painted alike—we used the same colors and our styles were similar, with free and open strokes, not tight lines. I gave her one of my paintings, a copy of that painting of an odd-looking house by van Gogh. One man, Buddy, used to come and watch us paint, and he bought a lot of my MBTA paintings of the old Orange Line stops at Dudley Street and Northampton Street. It's all torn down now. Marie Ugo has passed away, but she was a great teacher.

I found out about an art class taught in a big cafeteria at the Condon school on D Street on Tuesday and Thursday nights. I went there in all kinds of weather. There were maybe seven people in the class, including a whole family. Warren Woodworth was the teacher. He belonged to the School of the Museum of Fine Arts, and his paintings were a little different from mine — he was a lighter painter, and he did excellent portraits. He came around to encourage each of us while we painted. I started drawing and I said, "I can't draw!" But he looked at what I was doing and said, "You *can* draw." Another time, a woman in the class said, "Look what Eileen did!" I had painted a happy dog (for a change) in a doghouse. The woman was very impressed by how I had painted the folds in the canvas flap; they came out just right. She told me to never sell that painting, because it was so good. I still have it. Warren eventually retired and moved to the South, and I heard later that he had passed away.

Then I heard about Albert's class at the white Presbyterian church on Vinton Street. It was a big room, with some people there who were just starting to learn how to paint. I painted with Mr. Hancock, and together we exhibited our paintings at a restaurant in town, near the Symphony Hall MBTA stop. Everyone liked our paintings, and they made the restaurant look like a museum.

I used to paint ghettos, subway stations, the Irish famine. I also painted religious paintings, maritime scenes, and some pretty ones, like rural landscapes — deer in the woods, barns and fields. I painted the bus going by my old apartment, and my garden; an Indian village; a sinking ship from the Civil War days — a lot of different types of paintings. I even painted one of a sad-looking cat! My favorite colors are ultramarine blue and yellow.

As a child I lived up on a hill, in a nice stone house on a cobblestone street. But down below was an alley. I used to stand on top of the hill and look

107

at the spooky alley below. There were some old brick buildings where families lived that backed onto the alley. They had no lights in the hallways or out back. The image of those back halls and the lack of lights stayed with me. I know what it is to be poor, so when I painted, I wanted to put my feelings on canvas about poverty and injustice—things that are not right.

One day I was mad at somebody. And when I painted a painting in Sister Adelle's class, I made the sky look wild. Sister knew I was angry at someone! A painting is a good painting if when you look at it, you can feel what it is saying, like a painting of poverty. You can feel the hunger when you look at it. I wanted people to look at my paintings and feel the suffering, like of the starving cat or dog, and then after they feel something, to take action—go out and do something, like feed a stray cat. Sometimes people don't listen to me, but when I put it on canvas, then they see how I feel. With the paintings, they can see my feelings about what is important to me.

When I was young, I wanted to go to the Museum school, but I couldn't. I also wanted to be a doctor, but I was not good in math, and I went to a high school that didn't have books. But I always got an A in art. I got to go to art school in my non-credit art classes in South Boston. I got papers from all my teachers that said I attended their classes.

I sold twenty-six paintings in my life. I exhibited at the South Boston Library, the Laboure Center, the Curley Recreational Center, Cranberry Cafe, the church on Vinton Street, Massachusetts College of Art, the Hurley Building, a restaurant in town, the Center (a community building), and in windows at the Shawmut Bank. My favorite artists are still Vincent van Gogh and the Ash Can Painters because of their realism and the fact that they painted real people and people working in the fields.

Although I had a few friends in the area, I had to leave Old Colony in 2000 because the man upstairs played rap music all the time so I couldn't paint anymore or get any rest. I had lived there for nineteen and a half years. I'm happy I was able to take those classes. I live in a quiet place now — so maybe I can pick up a paintbrush again.

*Dudley Street MBTA, Roxbury*

# Love Stories

# LOVE AT
# THE YACHT CLUB

## *Ann E. DeSilva*

MY FATHER SERAFINO BRAZZO was born in Italy on June 14, 1901. He came to this country when he was one year old. My mother Katherine was born in New York, November 2, 1912. Both families came to South Boston on Vicksburgh Street. My parents both grew up there. They fell in love and were married in 1930.

I lived on I Street all my life, in my parents' house.

The best years of my life were the twenty years I was with my second husband, Joe. We met because my mother was invited to a wedding and a gathering at the bride's house afterward. I said, "Ma, you'll get a ride from all your relatives there." I wasn't invited. She said, "No. I'll feel better, Ann, if you come and pick me up." So I rang the bell on the South Boston Yacht Club and Joe opened the door. We started to chat (I was divorced ten years), and he invited me to a dinner with all his friends that he introduced me to, while I was waiting for my mother. In the meantime, my mother got a ride with her relatives and I was at the yacht club until two o'clock in the morning.

My husband was a good-looking man with dark hair, brown eyes, and perfect teeth. I fell in love with him about a month after we met. When he invited me down to the yacht club the second time, I told him I had a daughter and right away he said, "Bring her down." Well, needless to say, they hit it off. My daughter Debbie just loved the water and the club, and she and Joe became very close, which meant a great deal to me. I was a working mom and all my free time was spent with her.

My mother had no idea that I would meet someone that night, but soon they also got along. My Joe loved my daughter and mother.

We spent most of our time at the South Boston Yacht Club. Joe had no car so I convinced him to buy a boat. The name of the boat was *Deb-Ann-Joe*. It was a sport fisherman with the outriggers and all of that. His parents owned a boatyard down on First Street, between K and I, before the military took it over, so I thought he knew everything about boats. He said, "My father used to pay me to leave," so he didn't know much about boats. Joe enjoyed fishing, and so did I, but I would not bait hooks or take fish off hooks. I told him many times to go with the guys but he never left me.

Joe and I were on the entertainment committee of the yacht club. We had many formal parties, with gowns and suits — Memorial Day, Commodore's Ball, Opening Night, Fourth of July, Valentine's Party, Closing Night. Every event started with a fancy cocktail party in the commodore's locker with fancy drinks and lots of hors d'oeuvres: shrimp, meatballs, pizza bites — whatever the entertainment committee could think of to offer. The next part of the evening — dinner and dancing — was held upstairs in the main ballroom. The tables were set with good china and centerpieces. The head table consisted of the officers and their wives; the women wore beautiful gowns and the men naval uniforms. The huge room was lit with nautical lanterns and of course a mirrored ball. We of-

ten had a live band, playing hits from Tony Orlando and Bobby Vincent. I had never danced with my first husband, but with Joe I danced my life right into his. He was a good dancer and we spent many nights under that disco ball.

I met Joe in 1972 and he passed on in 1985. He was so sweet, but he died at fifty-six of throat cancer. And it's been twenty years. I'll never meet anyone else like him. When he passed on, I couldn't handle the boat so I had to sell it, but I am still a member of the South Boston Yacht Club. I have a beautiful locker right on the water, where my door is always open to friends. It has a futon, fridge, microwave, coffeepot, and a big window looking right out onto the ocean. I spend a lot of time there, knitting, socializing, and remembering the good times.

# A FRIEND THAT HELPED
# CHANGE MY LIFE

## *Barbara Knight*

AFTER BEING IN BOSTON for a few months, things started to fall apart between me and my mother, with whom I lived. I found myself looking for an apartment for me and my children. I had very little income and did not know the city very well. A man named Jackson whom I did not know, although he recognized me from my teen years, found me an apartment. Not only did Jackson find the apartment, he helped me financially until I could do for me and my kids.

Being young, I thought he had an ulterior motive for helping. I thought he wanted a different kind of relationship and I thought he wanted to move in with me. How wrong I was. He shared a house with his brother and sister-in-law. I also found out this sister-in-law would send food sometimes to make sure the kids were not hungry. He always said that she had "cooked too much," but I knew better.

He owned a truck and was sort of a collector: some junky stuff, some good stuff. Anything he thought I could use — furniture, clothes, appli-

117

ances—he would bring to us. I bought a children's toolbox for the kids. I did not think any of the tools in that box would be able to cut through anything. How wrong I was. I don't know which one of my boys (or both) decided to try the saw on the table leg. Little by little they sawed a part of the table leg off. I did not notice the shrinking leg until it fell down. Of course, my sons were nowhere to be found, even though they were always the first in the kitchen, ready to eat. When I asked about the table, no one knew what happened. The boys said the girls did it—I knew the girls did not do it. A few days later, Jackson came to visit. Since the kitchen was his favorite place, he noticed that I did not have the table. His first question was, "What happened to the table?"

I told him, "Ask the boys." The boys said Jackson cut the table leg because they saw his saw in the truck. A few days later, Jackson brought me a table with two chairs. The legs were metal. When I asked him why he and his family helped us so much, he would always say, "The kids." He said someone helped his family and they were grateful, so he helped mine. He asked only two things from me: first, that he would be able to visit sometimes, and second, that when he did, to have the coffee pot on the stove. Because of this man and his family, I made the decision to help people, especially children—a decision I have never regretted. Because of that decision, I am a mother of twelve kids, seven of my own, five of other people's—none adopted. They came to visit and never went home.

Being a mother of seven kids one would think I had enough to worry about, but along came John who reminded me of Jackson and his family. John was my godson and had a twin sister. His mother left him at home alone a lot. He always seemed to have a runny nose. She couldn't be bothered with having to wipe his nose often. The day I got him, he had been

left alone all day. This was when police and social workers did not take kids out of homes easily. When I saw him with his diaper hanging down from having it on all day, and a tear-stained face, I told his mother if she didn't want him, to give him to me. She reached into the crib and handed him to me. He was around a year and a half. Now he is forty-three and still my baby. He is a good father to his kids.

His relationship with his mother is not very good. He has tried through the years to have a mother-son relationship. I have encouraged him but I believed him when he told me about a year ago that he would not try anymore. John opened the door for two more boys and two more girls.

The next child I brought in, Carol, was a friend of my daughter. She liked to visit and asked if she could come live with us. I said yes, but she had to ask her mother. I was joking but Carol was serious. Carol asked and her mother said yes; they were dealing with a family problem at that time. Carol stayed with my family until she became pregnant at which time she went home. About two months after the baby was born, she came back, baby and all, and stayed until she got her first apartment.

The next girl, Adrieene, came to live with us because she could not get along with her mother. She was fourteen years old at the time, and stayed with me until she got her apartment a number of years later.

My fourth child, Ronnie, came to live with us because his stepfather did not want him in the house. He is one that my kids suggested I take in. Last, my son Terrance came to live with me when he was thirteen. When I first met him, he was walking up and down the street I lived on at that time. He lied and said he was eighteen. I found out that he was only thirteen (a runaway). When he was admitted to the hospital, they were going to put him in a foster home. He lived with me until he moved to another state.

Jackson and his family changed my life and the lives of my children. I have been blessed, so blessed that it made me reach out and help other people. My life work of helping the less fortunate is the result of their kindness.

# DESTINATION UNKNOWN

## *Joseph R. Saia*

Tuesday, June 6, 1944

Dearest Millie,

It is 3:30 P.M. and I am still in Fort Devens. I am in the yard on a troop train. There are about eighteen cars and I am in the last one. There are twenty-eight fellows in each car. They have three beds, one on top of the other like in a ship. It gives one a funny feeling pulling out of here and not knowing where we are going. Don't worry about anything; the way the war is going now, the end should not be far away. Any moment now the train will be pulling out. All these fellows I am going with are new fellows. They just came into the Army. Only one fellow who went to cook school is with me, but he is in the car ahead of me. Boy, were we glad when we met. I believe we will be in the same camp. I hope so because he is a swell guy. Calling you up today was good. It made me feel that you were near just to listen to your voice. I can imagine Rosemarie staring into the telephone when she heard me calling her.

As we move out I will add more to this letter, but I won't be able to mail this until I get to camp. Wherever that is.

The train is pulling out now and we are on our way. You can see I am writing while the train is going, the way the writing is shaky.

Well, we reach over and pull towards the west, all you can see is hills and woods. You can see the mountains running on the side of the train. We are picking up speed now and the telegraph poles come by kind of quick. The train rattles as if someone was doing the rhumba. The train is kind of quiet except for a few fellows singing and playing the harmonica; it is good to hear. We must be going about sixty miles an hour now. Just went by Fitchburg, Massachusetts, and we keep going on. In the towns, people wave as we go by. And stare at us. I bet they have someone in the service, too.

We had chow. Frankfurters and beans, fruit cocktail, and four slices of bread. This country is mostly dairy farms; you see plenty of cows. We just passed Hoosick Falls at 7:15 P.M. And we still roll west. There are plenty of valleys and the sun is still shining and all the boys are looking outside. They seem like a nice bunch of fellows. While I look out right now I see a pretty valley with a lot of farms. We must be crossing into New York state. If one does not travel, one will never realize how big a country we have with all the farms, orchards, and dairies. We reached Troy, New York, at 7:45 and stopped in the middle of the city, right in the street. We were there for fifteen minutes while kids ran up to the train and we threw money to them. You should see those kids run for that money; this is the poorest part of the city. I threw twenty-five pennies to the kids; they must have been four, five, six, or seven years old. When they got the money, they were all smiles.

The porter is making beds now. Well, good night, sweetheart. And God bless you and the baby. Goodnight my dears and we roll on. I still don't know where. Keep your chin up.

Millions of kisses and hugs,
Your loving husband,
Joe

~

Wednesday, June 7, 1944
5:30 A.M.

Good morning, darling Millie,

Riding on this train is no picnic. Trying to sleep, you bounce up and down until the motion puts you to sleep. Philadelphia is big; as I look out there are plenty of factories here and all are smoking away as far as the eye can see.

~

While getting chow we crossed into Delaware. At 6:45 A.M. we passed Newark. This country is all farms and you can see corn growing. I always wanted to travel, but never knew I would do it at Uncle Sam's expense. Don't worry, I am going to see everything I can and tell you all about it when I come home. There is one relief in my mind that you have a nice home and our baby to keep you busy and your mother to live with you and this takes a load off my mind. Don't think for a moment that I am not thinking about you because I write this way.

Here we are going through some farms now and you can see horses running around and I wish Rosemarie could see them. I wish my dad could be here with me to see this country we are going through. And we roll on destination unknown.

‿

A train just whizzed by and then goes *wham! Whiz, Wham!* What a noise. Right behind us is a train full of WAVES [Women Accepted for Volunteer Emergency Service]. It is about ten minutes on our tail, and all the boys look back trying to get a glimpse of them. All I can see now are trees and farms and, oh, boy, the sun just came out and it is nice and warm just like you hugging me. Some thought, eh! And we roll on and on, destination unknown. The fellows are singing and playing the harmonica and it is cheerful.

‿

As we pulled out of Baltimore along the tracks the workers stopped their work to wave at us. You know, as we move south you can see a lot of colored people doing all kinds of work. It is 9:15 A.M. and all we have to do is look out the window, where it seems all the world is made of trees.

We are still in Maryland; just stopped at Riverdale and it is 10:00 A.M. now. Another troop train passed us and we waved back. They looked like they were going overseas. They were wearing combat clothes — well good luck to them. May God watch over us.

I still haven't had a chance to buy a paper.

‿

We crossed the Potomac River and now I'm in Virginia. We pulled into a railyard and are taking on water and a new engine. We have been here a half-hour and we should have chow pretty soon. Every time we reach a different rail company we switch crews and the engine and we get banged forward and back. This is a smoky yard full of coal dust flying around.

⟿

We are running near a river or the ocean I cannot tell. If it is the ocean, we are still going south. It could be Chesapeake Bay. That's what it looks like.

Is there no stopping this train? We just keep on going. When I look at the map that is in my mind, and see Boston on it, I can begin to see that it will be a long time before I come home again. Just write to me every day, write anything you do during the day. The smallest things you do. That is what I like to read. Tell me about Rosemarie, my father, Ma, your mother, my brothers, and your family, or something that happens around them. Tell me about my garden and how the plants grow. Tell me how fresh Rosemarie is and how nice she is. Tell me about yourself. Don't worry about anything, I can take care of myself. With God's helping and watching over us the day will come when we are together again.

⟿

3:00 P.M. and we are pulling into Richmond, the capital of Virginia. You can see where the colored people live near the tracks in shacks and old houses. I saw where they store tobacco, Edgeworth Tobacco Company. Beyond the tracks seem to be better houses.

We are still in Richmond station and there's a freight train with about twenty cars of watermelons making my mouth water. This is the land that makes watermelons. I liked that watermelon you had Saturday.

Going by Raleigh Cigarettes — they have plenty of tobacco curing. You should have seen the two cute little calves, they were so small and they were eating grass.

Just had chow 6:00 P.M. Pork chop, one potato and some stewed tomatoes, a pear, three slices of bread, and a cup of coffee. While I was getting through with chow we crossed into the town of Wise, North Carolina. Pa should see this, with all the wheat and oats growing here it looks like Mineo. There is plenty of corn planted here, too.

7:15 P.M. We are leaving Franklinton, North Carolina, and we roll on and on destination unknown. I am looking inside the shacks. They are supposed to be houses and inside are sickening sights, dirty, all one family together. And we are trying to make a better world for Europe while we close our eyes at home. As I understand all the land is worked by sharecroppers and the banks and insurance companies own the land.

7:45 P.M. The sun shines yet. We pulled into Raleigh, North Carolina, and we are at the station now. Kids are running up to the train, barefoot. They all have the southern drawl. This is the capital of North Carolina. As we pull out of the city you see that the whites live in shacks, too. What a poor lot down here.

Thursday, June 8, 1944

Dearest sweetheart,

Good morning. 6:00 A.M. Slept alright last night, the swaying and the banging put me to sleep. Awoke about 3:30 A.M. and was going through Chester, South Carolina. Looked up and what a beautiful moon — you know what you call a lover's moon — and went back to sleep again thinking about you. A few more bangs and swayings and was fast asleep until 6:00 A.M. and we're going through Greenwood, South Carolina. I never heard so many roosters crowing.

7:30 A.M. Well, honey, we are rolling along to our destination and it won't be long now. I haven't read a paper this morning and do not know anything about the invasion. I pray it is a success.

7:45 A.M. Littleton. We crossed into Georgia and we still go on and on. We stopped at a small town called Alberton for water and the colored kids all ran to the side of the train. They dance and sing. They have no shoes or stockings and have old patched clothes. We threw money to them and you should see the kids scramble for the money. Here comes a little colored fellow the size of Angelo and he has his foot wrapped up. He must have hurt it and stands away from the other kids. I called him and he came to the window of the car. I gave him a nickel; you should see him smile. I asked him his name and he said George, Jr. He has a little patched bathrobe as old as the hills, and that is all the clothes he has. Living conditions down here are deplorable from what I have seen. Now we are pulling out; as the train goes by the farms you see women washing clothes in tubs by hand. You see colored farmers with mules plowing between the corn. Wheat fields as far as the eye can see make me think of my father's wheat field.

Colbert, Georgia. 10:15 A.M. We are leaving this jerk town and we roll on and on.

Atlanta, Georgia

2:00 P.M. Here I am at an orchard—there must be thousands of peach trees. You hear of the expression, "Georgia peaches." The earth down here is a reddish color. In some of the farms they are threshing either wheat or oats. You can see them cut and bundle it. There are quite a few big cotton mills down here.

And we keep going on. There is a house like in *Tobacco Road,* the movie; the same thing, that picture did not exaggerate at all. Here it is 3:30 P.M. and it makes forty-eight hours since we started; some ride. When I want exercise I walk to the back and look out, and watch the country. My dad would enjoy these wheat fields. The wheat is stacked up after it is threshed, just like he used to do.

We must be going about fifty miles an hour. The farmers work the field with mule and harness like my dad had, or by tractors, but mostly by mule. They have straw hats. My dad used to work like this.

Well, we are getting there in about forty minutes. This time for sure. Camp Wheeler, Georgia. Destination reached. Arrived safe and sound, thank God, at 6:30 P.M.

Your loving husband,
xxxx Joe xxxxx

# Mysterious Ways

# FINDING TONY

## *Mary E. Clarke*

THIS IS IN HONOR of my son, Anthony Ray Clark, a veteran of the U.S. Marine Corps. He enlisted against my wishes. His father said that he would be fine and it would make a man out of him. He was only eighteen when he enlisted in the late 1950s. Anthony was a proud and dedicated Marine. He would always say that no other branch of the armed services was as special as being a Marine.

His graduation in North Carolina was such a very special day for the parents and their sons. My husband and I stayed at a hotel near the base. The only thing that seemed out of place was when the employees at the hotel saw that I was African American. I was the first. The maids all came to my room to take a look and ask if I was some official or something. I said no, that I was just there to see my oldest son graduate.

When I found out what all the fuss was about, I learned that my being there had allowed all African Americans to come to see their sons go off and fight for this country. It was so funny to my son. He said that his drill sergeant told him, "Your mother has really stirred up this whole base — a real declaration for everyone." My son was so proud of being a Marine and happy about me breaking an old code.

When he came home for seven days before being shipped to Vietnam, it broke my heart because he had to leave Thanksgiving Day. It was confirmed by his orders.

Some time later, I saw reports in the newspaper, on TV and radio that so many of our young boys were being killed. I was always afraid for my son. There seemed to be no solution to the senseless war. The fact of the matter was, no one in Washington had any of their sons or daughters in this war.

One day I received a special letter saying that Anthony had been hurt and was being shipped to a hospital in Hawaii. I called every day and was told that he would be able to talk to me on the third day. I was so very happy to hear his voice. He said that he had been in a place with heavy losses of life on both sides. When he was able, in a couple of months, he was back fighting again. His letters home said, "I must go back. Many of my friends are there dying and some are hurt."

I hated every minute of every hour of every day that my son was away. Then the day came when he went missing. I thought I would just die. My only hope was to pray and ask the Lord to protect him and let him be okay.

One night, months later, I was watching the news of the war, when coming down a hill were five vets carrying guns. My son was wearing an old fishing hat that his dad had given him before he left for Vietnam. I screamed, "Oh God, it's him, it's my Tony!"

I called the Defense Department in Washington to tell them about the picture I saw on television and in a few days he and his buddies were found. God must have protected them because there were so many bombs in the fields and so many explosives. My son was leading the group and later told everyone that I helped him. "Each step I took I would hear her say, 'No, stop, go slow, to your left.' " He said, "She carried us to safety."

Anthony came home but was in and out of the hospital. He was declared 100 percent mentally disabled, but it was okay because he had been to hell and still came back. I could smile again.

Now I am sad once more because he is gone. He passed away after a long battle with cancer, but it is okay because he is home now with God and there is no more pain and suffering. He allowed himself to smile when there was nothing to smile about. When he lost his leg and had a stroke, he wasn't bitter because he was still a proud Marine who fought to make the world a better place for his daughter and family.

# GODPARENTS
# BEARING GIFTS

## *Jenna Fitzgerald*

WHEN I WAS YOUNG, life was good and we had no complaints. As far as my brother and I were concerned we had everything. The one thing I couldn't understand was why at my brother's birthday parties he always received gifts from his godparents. As far as I knew I didn't have godparents and I accepted that.

My tenth birthday was approaching and Mum told me she had a big surprise for me. I thought great, my birthday party and my godparents are coming and bearing gifts. I was speechless when mum told me her big surprise: She was going to have a baby.

September 8, 1938, came and I had a new baby sister and she had two godparents bearing gifts. Much as I loved my sister I resented godparents bearing gifts.

When it came time for my confirmation, my sister came down with the very contagious scarlet fever. In those days the Board of Health was notified right away so they could quarantine your home. A skull and crossbones (paper) was attached to your front door and no one was to go in or out. I was sent to my grandmother—wink, wink—so I could go to school. I just couldn't miss my confirmation after all the training I had been through with my class, and not only that, it only happened every three years. I would die if I had to miss it!

My thoughts were on the white dresses and veils all the girls would be wearing, and maybe my godparents were going to surprise me and show up for the occasion.

Confirmation day was finally here. Through Mum's tears I was dressed in my finery and sent off with love and kisses to make the long walk all by myself up to the Gate of Heaven Church.

With a heavy heart I took my place in the pew to go through the ceremony by rote. I couldn't stop thinking, *Everyone here has family here to see them, but not me. I'll even bet they all have godparents here, but not me. Poor, poor me.*

Then the music soared and the ceremony was over. We soldiers of God lined up behind the bishop and up the center aisle we marched, right to the massive front doors of the Gate of Heaven Church. Outside the families were waiting for their special confirmed child. I had no one. As I stood at the door I looked to the left and waved and then to the right and waved, then straight ahead and pointed (to no one) and mouthed, "I'm coming!" Then I ran down the stairs crying my head off and ran all the way home. A day I have remembered all of my life.

Mum was waiting in the window as I ran down the street to our house. I could see her crying and it made me feel worse. I got hugs and kisses and sweet talk but it didn't take the pain away knowing no one came to see me. Not even my godparents.

JENNA FITZGERALD - SOUTH BOSTON

I asked Mum to solve the mystery for me: Why weren't they there? She told me that after the christening, my godparents left for Europe on an extended vacation and hadn't returned. I think mum kissed the Blarney stone more than once.

⟳

The years flew by and my thoughts changed to high school dances, boys, and more boys. I very rarely if ever gave a thought to godparents, even though all my siblings had godparents bearing gifts on birthdays and holidays. *Poor, poor me.*

The next time it crossed my mind that maybe I was never baptized (that is why no godparents) was when I was preparing for my wedding. So I went to my mother and said, "Mum, you have to level with me; I have to know if I was truly baptized and had godparents." This is her story: "Darling, of course you were baptized. Your father and I were having tough times like everyone else with the Depression going on when you were born. Usually in our day the baby was christened right away, as the mother never took the child out until they were christened. We didn't have the money to have a big show and your father was too proud to let his family know how desperate we were. After two weeks I put my foot down and said, "This baby will be christened now, no more excuses." Dad went down to the local pub and got a fellow and his lady friend to come home with him and set the arrangements for you to be christened that weekend." That they were simply acquaintances and not close friends explains why there was no communication over the years. At least this beats the story Mum told me when I was a kid.

Life went on and I had a beautiful wedding and never gave a thought to my no-show godparents. My marriage was blessed with six beautiful children and, as of now, fifteen grandchildren and one great-grandchild. My husband and I enjoyed fifty-two wonderful years of marriage until he passed away in 1999.

As I read his memory card we passed out at the wake, the words hit me like a ton of bricks. "I'll be waiting for you, for a time, until we meet again in Heaven." The old fear surfaced again. What if by some crazy circumstance I really was not baptized? Then I could never get to heaven. I panicked and all logic left me.

I confided in my oldest daughter and she alleviated my fears. In a very knowing way she pointed out the fact that one sacrament follows the other and there was no way I could have been married in the Catholic Church if I had not received all the other sacraments. Of course I knew that—why had I panicked again? Old age I guess.

My daughter, in her wisdom and to settle me down once and for all, took it upon herself to go to the Gate of Heaven rectory where she figured I had to have been baptized. No record. She knew I had lived on Fourth Street near the firehouse when I was a baby, so she figured the parish was Gate of Heaven. No record.

In a panic, she went to Saint Brigid rectory and sure enough the record was there: "Virginia was baptized in April 1928 and her godparents were a Mr. Madden and a Mary Alice Martin."

I was so relieved to finally be certain I had godparents and I was baptized. I was so grateful to these two strangers that I had a thank-you Mass said for them. As it says on my husband's headstone: "All is well. We will meet again."

# SISTER DEATH

## *Louise Taglieri*

DEATH WAS A PART of my life from an early age, but to me, it was not morbid. Growing up in the North End, death was considered much more a part of life than it seems to be now. When someone passed away, the wake was held at home. You'd know there was a wake in the neighborhood when you saw a huge black wreath hung in the doorway. As children, we'd go to these wakes even though we didn't always know who'd died. We'd hear that a person was forty or fifty, and as children we'd think that was so old.

The wakes were held in the parlor. You'd take out all the furniture and wake the body for three days. Because the body could never be left alone, someone was always on watch: the women during the day and the men at night.

I remember one neighbor's passing; she lived on the third floor. They had to carry the casket up three flights of stairs and back down. There used to be a tradition of opening the casket at the cemetery for the family to have a final look, but since the body could get jostled badly with all the stairs, they stopped that tradition.

Not only were the wakes held at home, but that's where the undertaker came as well. As a child, I was witness to a body being prepared for burial. We lived on the third floor, and had a fire escape from which we could see what went on in the building across from ours. One of the men in that building had died, and I was on the fire escape when the undertaker came. I watched, mesmerized, as they washed the body, drained the fluids into a basin and embalmed the body, then finally dressed it. I wasn't scared at all, just fascinated.

The wake and the trip to the cemetery were honored traditions in our community. It is an important part of our culture to be surrounded by friends and relatives while grieving. From the age of two and continuing throughout my life, Memorial Day has been a special day of remembrance of my loved ones, a holy day for deceased family members. I remember what a great time we had during these trips to the cemetery, even as two- and three-year-old children.

Our funeral director would hire a bus to take us to the Saint Michael's Cemetery in Roslindale, and pick us up about five hours later for our return home. My mother, grandmother, dad, grandpa, and all the members of the family would make the trip. When I was two, they had a special reason to grieve. My mother, then nineteen, gave birth to my baby brother, and a few months later, my grandmother at forty-eight had a "change-of-life baby" and my uncle was born. These two sons died of illness within a few months of each other and were buried in their own plots, close to each other. It was a double grief and my mother and grandmother consoled each other for having lost their sons to Sister Death.

But God had other plans to ease the pain of their sorrow. Mom became pregnant again and had a baby girl she named after my Grandma Jenny.

And lo and behold, Grandma was pregnant and had a baby boy. Miracle of miracles!

Anyway, back at the cemetery, while the adults tended the flowers on the graves, we children were assigned a play area away from the gravesites where we could play to our hearts' delight. Close by, the cardboard boxes that had held the flowers were discarded in a designated area. We would take the boxes and use them as sleds to slide down the mounds of dirt. We had at least twelve or fifteen children playing together. Oh, what a time we had. While our parents were grieving, we called it a picnic! Our memories were not of sorrow, just an important part of our culture.

As an adult, to this day I have never missed going to the cemetery at least three or four times a year. Now it is Mother's Day, Father's Day, Easter, and Christmas. We change the flowers as the seasons come and go. I also encourage my children to visit the cemetery, but I fear that this tradition is dying out. Just as the wake is now not in the home but at a funeral parlor, and for one day not three, and the reception is usually a catered affair at a hall or restaurant rather than at home. There are also more cremations now. Sometimes I wonder why we do not adopt the Roman ways of burying the deceased. In Italy, there are catacombs where for two thousand years the same procedure is observed: After a period of ten years post-burial, the oldest male in the family "cleans the bones" of the deceased member and stacks them in the wall of the crypt. This tradition has solved the problem of space, while in the U.S. and other parts of Europe, we always need more land to establish another cemetery.

To end on a humorous note, here's a story of my mother accusing me of dancing on my father's grave. Mom loved to "take a ride" and visit the cemetery. Our family gravesite is adjacent to the road. On our last visit,

I parked in the "middle of the road," according to her. Mom was angry with me. She accused me of parking too far from the site. I stamped my feet and said, "Do you want me to park on the grave?!" Upon seeing this, Mom accused me of "dancing on my father's grave." To her dying day, she never asked me again to "go for a ride to the cemetery."

# The Value of Family

# "CLAIR DE LUNE"

## *Daisy Janey*

B Y  T H E  T I M E  I was ten or thereabout, I was allowed to take the streetcar to Everett Station where I boarded the elevated train to Northampton Street in Roxbury to visit my aunt and cousins on Hammond Street. (The streetcars were replaced by the trolley which was essentially a bus that got its power from overhead wires. The trolley had a pole that connected to the overhead powerline. This provided mobility and allowed the trolley to pull over to the curb to pick up and dispense passengers. On more than one occasion, the pole became unhitched from the overhead power source and the trolley conductor would have to get out and reattach it.)

My aunt lived in a small apartment on the second floor of a brick row house. The compact kitchen was the center of life, and it revolved around a large black iron stove that was fueled with coal around the clock. It provided heat and hot food. The coal came in a supersized brown paper bag, which was emptied into a metal hod sitting on the floor.

It was a tight squeeze, but everyone ate in the kitchen: Aunt Lottie, cousins Emmet and Sara, and me. The policy that children should be seen and not heard was strictly enforced, so I listened a lot (but why Auntie's last name was Harris and Emmet and Sara's was Simpson, I never learned).

Emmet and Sara were older than I and had jobs; Emmet was a pharmacist at a large Roxbury drugstore, and Sara worked for a real estate agency. Auntie kept house and cooked luscious meals, served always with the most delicious lemonade I ever tasted then or since.

Each of them had a small bedroom, and bricks heated on the stove and carefully wrapped in towels were placed under the blankets to warm their beds in the cold rooms. The only other room was the parlor. The centerpiece of that room was an upright piano. A potbellied woodstove sat in one corner and a Victrola in another. When my aunt took me to visit her friends, I found that just about every family had a piano in the parlor. Music was very important in the average black family.

Someone once said, "Home is where they have to take you in when you have nowhere to go." Aunt Lottie's cluttered apartment gave me a sense of home. Being a relation, I experienced a feeling of safety and belonging there. Her familiar southern cooking fed my body and music from the piano fed my soul, for Sara's newly acquired husband was a musician and an accomplished pianist. One song he played for me over and over again was "Clair de Lune" by Claude Debussy. I could not get my fill and eventually took enough piano lessons later in life to play a simplified version. The melody still moves me to silent tears.

# LESSONS FROM
# MY PARENTS

## *Barbara Maldero*

Growing up, my parents were a great influence on me. They taught me many lessons that I have never forgotten and have tried to pass on to my own children and grandchildren. Here are just a few that stay in my mind.

My father was the educator, always reading a newspaper or books. He was a tinsmith but you would never know it from his appearance; he was always well-dressed, with a newspaper under his arm. He was self-educated, loved to read and write, and went to the library often. He instilled in his children that reading was an important part of our lives. So much so that he banned funny books (comics) from the house — but we snuck them in anyway.

My mother was the heart and soul of the family. I remember her as a lady: gentle, warm, and understanding, never loud or outspoken, always trying to solve whatever we thought was a problem. Her life was cooking, cleaning, and sharing her love for her ten children. She would always tell us to be kind to everyone. She'd say, "It doesn't cost you anything to say hello

to people you meet," and, "All the money in the world can't buy you love or the respect you earn from others."

My first remembrance of my parents was teaching us to always share what we had, especially with those who were in need. We didn't have much, being a family of ten children (seven boys and three girls), but what we had was love for everyone. It is part of my life today by being involved in my community, which I feel is part of my heritage.

I remember as a little girl being taught to pray for those who were in need and to always be there for whatever the need may be. Today, being much older and hopefully wiser, I have tried to instill in my children and grand-children the value of understanding other people's needs. For example, for the past twenty years (since retiring from BlueCross BlueShield), I have been directing the Saint Damien's Society volunteer group at Saint Leonard's Church. We began as the Catholic Medical Mission, sending supplies to third-world hospitals. The first thing we did was to make john-nies from men's shirts, and from sheets we made bandages by the thou-sands. When U.S. soldiers were in Saudi Arabia, we heard they needed paperback books. We filled cartons with donated books, and in fact the boy who helped me send them is now a priest (Michael Della Penna). Af-ter the Oklahoma City bombing, I called to find out which hospital the children had been sent to, and we sent hug-a-bears to them, along with all our prayers for healing.

Now we knit and crochet blankets, hats, and scarves for those in need, as well as sewing teddy bears for children who may not have any. Some of the organizations we send packages to include the Dana Farber Can-cer Institute, the Shriner's Burn Center, the Perkins School for the Blind, Rosie's Place, Bridge Over Troubled Water, Saint Mary's House for Un-wed Mothers, Children's Hospital, the Home for Little Wanderers, Fran-ciscan Brothers of the Poor, and many nursing homes.

Saint Francis said, "It is in giving of ourselves that we receive." And what we receive in this case is the satisfaction of having people know that they are being thought of. Their thanks is all we need, and you should see all the letters we get — we could cover a whole wall with them. One of my favorites is from the Perkins School — the kids traced their hands and put their names on them. Another child, who received a hug-a-bear, drew her bear which she had named "Gooba — my bear I got. From Katie." The Temporary Home for Women also sent a beautiful handmade card with colorful cutouts of houses and people holding hands. All these people knew we were thinking of them, just as my parents taught us to.

*My father with my brother (and his newspaper).*

# FAMILY VALUES

## *Rita (Palermo) Mulkern*

T HE VALUES I was brought up with were religion, family, and education. In all three, my grandmother Corinne Pizzano played a significant part.

Since my grandmother's house was across the street from the school (Saint John's) and the Italian Catholic church (Sacred Heart), my family knew all the priests. Father Louis Savio used to call my grandmother. When I called up to her window, "Grandma, I want a penny for candy!" he'd call over, "Grandma, I want a new pair of shoes, please!" And she'd get him a pair. Also, if she made two pizzas, she'd send me over with one for him. The priests always came to my grandmother's house for a "good meal" and some of her homemade wine. (She and my father both came from an area outside of Naples known for its wine.)

My father, like most Italian men, attended church only for weddings, funerals, and christenings. However, he was also friendly with all the pastors and priests; he respected them. On many occasions, I would be sent over to the rectory with a gallon of his homemade wine and a box of candy. On holidays I would bring the church plants (Easter lilies, roses, etc.) from the florist my father owned with his brother (Palermo Brothers). Also on Easter, Thanksgiving, and Christmas, the priests would come and bless the house with holy water. They'd sit with the family and sometimes stay for dinner or cordials and pastry.

My favorite priest was Reverend Mario Tardivo. He came to the Sacred Heart parish as a young priest and became pastor twice. (He went to serve as an Army chaplain, then returned.) My girlfriend Elena and I used to swing on the iron church gates and Reverend Mario would say, *"Via! Via!"* which means "Scram!" I tagged him Father Via. The people of the North End gave him a big eightieth birthday party. Many, many parishioners attended. He recently passed away, but I used to always send him a card at Christmas, signed "Via Via."

I was also fond of Reverend Savio, who became the pastor of Sacred Heart. He married my husband John and me in 1956. When I was teaching at Saint John's School, he would enter the building and chaos would ensue; the children all loved him very much. He passed away many years ago and was waked at Sacred Heart before they returned his body to his family in Italy for burial.

My mother was a quiet woman of great faith. Unlike my father, she attended church regularly. On Mondays she attended Sacred Heart Novena to the Blessed Mother. On Tuesdays she went to Saint Leonard's for services about Saint Anthony. On Wednesdays she went to Saint Mary's Church to hear the "good news" about Saint Francis Xavier. On Sundays she always went to the nine o'clock Mass with my brother and me, after which he and I attended Sunday school at Saint John's under the direction of the Sisters of Saint Joseph. (Years later I taught at Saint John's as a reading specialist.)

At Sacred Heart, we'd make a donation, light the red candles, and say a prayer. When I bring my granddaughter there now, the candles are electric because of the fire hazard.

Besides respect for the priests and church attendance, we were taught respect for family time. At suppertime, which was six o'clock on weekdays and two o'clock on Sundays, promptness and cleanliness were the rules. There was no fooling at the table. We kids had to talk about what we had learned in school that day. Dinnertime was a gathering of information about *all* the family, including uncles, aunts, cousins, etc. — who was doing what, who was going to school, who was graduating, who was engaged, who was getting married.

But that's not all: Every Saturday, my mother and my aunts had to go to my grandmother's house to check in. They had to bring their spouses and children. My grandmother would be sitting on the front stoop with friends, waiting for us to arrive. You'd be in *serious* trouble if you didn't show up. She'd cook for the family. After dinner the men would leave and the "girls" would sit there crocheting and gossiping. I'd push the babies in the carriages.

My grandmother was way ahead of her time, especially for a foreign-born citizen who never learned to speak English. She was very fashionable, always dressed with a hat, gloves, stockings, and good shoes, ready to go out. She was very gregarious and therefore had many friends and acquaintances in the North End. A successful businesswoman, my grandmother ran a restaurant and bought two buildings with her profits. (At her place, Pizzano's, at 6 Moon Street, you could get a dish of spaghetti with two meatballs, a slice of bread, and a glass of my grandfather's wine for twenty-five cents.)

She and I had a special relationship. I was the only grandchild allowed to pump and play her mahogany player piano. And for twenty years I was the one who administered her daily insulin. I used to love to go to her house. She was always making pizza or baking cookies, and I'd watch her

make the "gravy" for the spaghetti. If I was naughty, my grandmother would speak to my mother and inform her that she was not to administer any punishment or *she'd* be in trouble. She'd always accompany my mother to the plays, pageants, and open houses at my school (the Eliot school, then Michelangelo). When I graduated from Girls High in 1947 she bought me a Smith Corona portable typewriter.

As I grew up, it was she who encouraged me to achieve my goal of going off to college. My uncles, being traditional, said it was a waste of money to send a girl to college, since I would just get married and have kids. My mother fit this mold; she was always at the sink or at the stove, cooking. She was an excellent cook, having learned from her mother. If my brother didn't like the meal she had prepared, she'd make another dish for him. She mostly stayed at home and lived a quiet life. But my grandmother had bigger ambitions for me. She told me to go to school, to strive, to become someone important. She was very proud to be at my college graduation from Northeastern University in 1953.

I had originally enrolled at Mount Ida Junior College in 1947, because of the interesting catalog. I won a medal in horseback riding and was happy there, but my father said I was to leave the school after one year because I wasn't "learning," only enjoying the athletic department. At Northeastern, I buckled down and became the president of Omega Sigma (the women's sorority) and class secretary. When I graduated in 1953, I decided to stay at the school and go on for a master's in education, which I obtained in 1955. I began my teaching career in Dedham, left to raise my three children, then taught in the Boston schools for almost twenty more years.

My husband and I met at Northeastern, and we stressed the value of education in raising our three children. (My husband John is the author of three books and taught at Babson College for thirty years.) All the kids attended Boston Latin, one son graduated from the University of Pennsylvania, and my daughter graduated from Harvard and the Northeastern School of Law. Wouldn't Grandma be proud!

# Living History

# A STRANGE
# COINCIDENCE

## *Peg Fahey*

SEPTEMBER 11, 2001. The day was calm. I was dressed and off to Ward Six, Precinct Four at the Gate of Heaven School hall to be the election clerk officer for voting. I'm the youngest of eight children (seven girls and one brother Paul) who all went to the Gate of Heaven School in South Boston.

At the beginning of the day at six o'clock, I write in the city clerk log all that are present and the police officers' names, then check all the voting machines to see that they are all set to zero and working properly. If not, we call city hall to come repair the machine. We have pink slips for Republican machines, blue for Democrats, and green sheets to file for independent voters.

Voting opens at seven o'clock. The morning was going fine till around nine thirty, when someone came in to tell us New York was hit by two planes that came from Logan Airport. (I heard later that two of those cells in the planes lived around the corner from me on Boston Street near Andrew Station.) I was in shock! I wrote in the clerk's book for the City of Boston, "Where is our security?"

By a strange coincidence, in this same building on December 7, 1941, my sister Mary's debating class for the Gate of Heaven School debated that this country couldn't be attacked, and their team won the debate. That very day we were attacked at Pearl Harbor by the Japanese. (Incidentally, my father was present at this debate. He was in World War I and took four bullets on the front lines in Arras, France — the last one left out of his platoon. He was a sergeant machine gunner in the Army.)

Here I am working till nine o'clock. (Governor Swift did not close anything, except airplanes were all grounded). Later that evening I went to Steve Lynch's rally; his speech was so appropriate at the time and helped to calm the hundreds of people there. He really was the man to be our congressman. Presently, I don't feel very secure about anything. Your safety, your health, your home. We are all here to be neighbors and take care of one another.

# MATTAPANNOCK MEMORIES

## *Nina Hayes*

VALENTINE'S DAY 1976 was a Saturday. It was sunny and clear with the temperature just below freezing. The hard-packed snow, sprinkled liberally with sand, crunched under my boots as I walked up the path to the Church of Saint Matthew and the Redeemer. The February meeting of the Mattapannock Woman's Club was at two o'clock and I was going to get my first peek at this group that I read about each week in the *South Boston Tribune*. I anxiously checked my clothes for baby food stains and diaper fuzz. Members of the Mattapannock Club were mature, accomplished South Bostonians. I was a twenty-something stay-at-home mother of two still working on my undergraduate degree in education.

Paula Fleming, my sponsor and treasurer of the club, met me at the door. We went downstairs where I was introduced to several members who offered to take my hat, coat, and boots. At the entrance to Grace Hall, a striking, silver-coiffed woman in a colorful fuchsia and forest green plaid suit asked me to sign the guest book. Lively chatter spilled from the hall. As I looked around, I saw a couple of members by the podium having what looked like a serious conversation. Then laughter drew my attention to the back of the hall where ten or more women buzzed around a large banquet table like bees at a hive. Two swinging doors on either side of the back wall were in constant motion as women balanced teacups, silverware, napkins, and serving trays with incredible precision. Although it was 1976, I felt like I had stepped back to another place in time.

Paula suggested we take a seat near the front of the hall so I wouldn't miss any detail of my first Mattapannock meeting. Chairs were arranged in six rows of five seats to a row on each side. There was an aisle between the sixty chairs leading to the podium. We sat in the second row on the right-hand side leaving the front row for the club officers.

At exactly two o'clock, Mrs. Ann Blaney, Mattapannock president, banged the gavel calling the meeting to order. She asked the members to stand to pledge allegiance to the flag. While we were still standing another member went to the piano and Martha Engler walked haltingly to the side of the podium, bent over, and snapped her leg brace in place for support. While she led us in a rousing version of "God Bless America," I was surprised by the lump in my throat when I realized how grateful I was to be an American.

When we were seated, Miss Alice DeWolfe, tall and slim wearing a bright red blazer, gave an invocation. The president then opened the business section of the meeting by calling each officer to the podium to give her report.

Quickly and efficiently the treasurer and secretaries read their reports. I couldn't help but notice how well-dressed and poised the officers were as I listened. Then I scanned the room and realized all the club members were dressed in various shades of pink or brilliant red for Valentine's Day! Af-

ter voting to accept the reports, the president introduced the chairman of the Education Committee to present the program of the day. Miss Claire Blaney gave a brief biography of the guest speaker.

Helen Dunne was a slight, gray-haired woman who looked out of place before her well-dressed audience. Club members wore hats that complemented their suits with pumps and matching handbags. Helen's plaid flannel shirt was tucked into her work pants that folded over her sturdy boots. Helen began by asking if any of the members could fire a rifle. Her question caught the group's attention and they chuckled and squirmed in their chairs. A lifelong resident of Peddocks Island in Boston Harbor, Helen described her daily routine. Without electricity or running water, life was hard on the island.

Helen was born in 1899, the year the Mattapannock was formed. This fact startled me because I recognized that many of the members were around her age but looked very different. She reflected on her childhood that was carefree yet had certain responsibilities. A one-room school on the island provided Helen and other resident children an education up to the sixth grade. Few took the ferryboat to Hull to go on to the upper grades. Fishing, farming, and chores filled her days.

Fort Andrews, active in harbor defense since 1904, was on the northeast side of the island. As a teenager, Helen would find any number of reasons to wander over by the fort. The sight of a young man in uniform took her breath away. When the women gave out a collective laugh, I was taken aback. It was hard to picture these impressive women as giggly teenagers swooning over young soldiers. World War I was being fought on another continent—what seemed to Helen a million miles away—but several of the soldiers told her vivid details of horrors on the western front that made it all too real and frightening.

At twenty-four, Helen married a fellow islander and eleven months later had her first son. Although it was difficult to eke out a living on the island, Helen and her growing family flourished. Her husband built a fishing dory and began a small business selling his catch to markets on the South Shore. He would bring newspapers, groceries, and store-bought pastries home from the mainland as treats for Helen. The Depression was on and this was the only way he could get payment for the fish. I watched as many of the women nodded in agreement.

When Pearl Harbor was attacked everything changed for Helen. Her son, only seventeen, enlisted in the Army. Fort Andrews intensified military activity on the island and many of the residents left for the mainland. Her husband's fishing was curtailed as rumors of German U-boat sightings circulated. As the war continued, Helen's life shifted like a riptide. Her son was killed on D-Day Three. The news took weeks to reach her. Struggling to keep the family healthy and safe, Helen's husband fished all night and farmed the rocky, sandy soil by day. Although the other three children could now help with duties and chores on the boat and on the island, Mr. and Mrs. Dunne never recovered from the news the Commander of Fort Adams brought them that perfect summer day in late June.

On her knees weeding pole beans, Helen remembered the frightening stories she had heard almost thirty years before from the soldiers based at Fort Adams. Over and over in her head she replayed the images of gunfire, trench warfare, poison gas, and exploding shells, praying her son was taken instantly without feeling fear or pain.

The members of the club were sympathetic to Helen's story because they too lost fathers, brothers, boyfriends, and relatives. Many of the Mattapannock women had important responsibilities during the war. All had endured tremendous hardship and lost loved ones, neighbors, and friends. I knew Helen Dunne had hit a raw nerve when I saw the tears in their eyes and the lace-edged hankies twisted in their hands. Although I was born years after World War I, I remembered the accounts my dad would tell me of his experiences in Europe and his brothers' in the Pacific. I became conscious of the shared pain that was unmistakably echoed in the absolute silence.

The quiet moment was broken when Helen slapped her rifle butt hard against the podium. "We all had to sacrifice to keep our country the greatest in the world!" she shouted.

Claire Blaney rose from her chair to thank Mrs. Dunne for her interesting program and invite the honored guest to join the members for tea. Each monthly program was followed by high tea usually with a theme. Eight members, acting as hostesses, arranged the lace cloths, washed teacups and saucers (before and after), prepared the food, and brewed coffee and tea.

I could not believe the banquet table at the other end of the hall. It reminded me of great Victorian feasts that I only read about in Brontë novels. Because it was Valentine's Day, the lace tablecloths were lined with pale pink to match the pale pearly roses in the centerpiece. At either end of the long table was an ornate sterling silver urn presided over by one of the tea hostesses. The elaborate potbellied urn gave off the delicious aroma of fresh brewed coffee, while the other decorative urn smelled of fragrant tea. Members and guests queued up to the hostess chatting nonstop with one another. Delicate pink cream cheese and cherry sandwiches, frosted hearty nut breads, and sugary sweets were displayed on gleaming silver or cut-glass trays. Helping myself to a carefully selected assortment of goodies, I stepped up to Debbie Reid, the hostess serving tea. Debbie's husband Doc was the headmaster of Southie High and a local historian who frequently presented a program for the Mattapannock Club. I almost dropped my teacup when Debbie offered to be one of my sponsors if I wanted to join the Club. I could barely respond with a timid, "thank you" and rushed to find a seat near Paula.

Looking back it's hard to believe I have been a member for over thirty years.

*Mattapannock* was the Native American name of South Boston. Loosely translated, it means a "sitting down" place. What started as a volunteer group of women rolling bandages for soldiers returning from the Spanish-American War in 1899 developed into a strong organization that provided support for veterans, service to the needy, and academic scholarships. Their good deeds and manners interlaced the South Boston community for more than one hundred years. As this bygone era comes to an end, I know my life was richer because of the influence of the Mattapannock women.

# WHATEVER IT TAKES FOR THEM TO ACHIEVE

## SOME POSITIVE AND NEGATIVE THOUGHTS ON THE BOSTON SCHOOL SYSTEM

## *Alice Hodge*

WHILE I WAS A STUDENT in the Boston school system, I encountered some teachers who demonstrated negativity toward me as a minority student. However, at home, my Moms and the rest of my family approached things from a positive perspective. This gave me the confidence and self-esteem I needed to succeed. For example, in one of my classes, each student was assigned a subject on which to prepare an oral presentation. I spent many afternoons at the Boston Public Library researching and preparing my assignment. On the date of my presentation I was thrilled because I knew the amount of work I had put into it and felt well-prepared. After giving my report I felt it had gone well; however, the teacher gave me a mark of C−. I was confused, but she did not take the time to show me where the report's weakness may have been.

My mother knew just how hard I had worked, and the time I had put into preparing the report. She had had to listen to me repeating the lines over

and over, to memorize them. So when hearing of the low mark, she didn't scold me but gave me a hug and said not to worry, I'd get a better mark next time.

Later that year, in this class, there appeared a teacher who was very stern but fair. On her first day, she walked in, hair in a tight bun, looking every inch the schoolmarm. Our first impression of her was far from glamorous, but as soon as she began teaching, the students perked up and a new feeling came over the class: this was a teacher we could learn from. I continued to participate in class as usual, doing my assignments and raising my hand. The teacher noticed this and pulled me aside one day to ask me what I was doing with a failing mark, to which I replied, "I don't know." She told me she would assign me certain chapters to read and then she would test me. I welcomed the chance to improve my grade and ended the year with a B+.

I grew up, married, and became the mother of two boys. Academically, things were fine until they reached middle school. Some of my friends and acquaintances had children the same age as mine. While attending a Home and School Association meeting at the school to check on the children's progress, I received negative information about my sons' academic performance — information that sounded familiar. As I checked with the other minority parents, I found that they had received the same information about their kids: mainly that they weren't up to the standard to be enrolled in the college prep course that we all wanted for our children.

As parents, we had to express ourselves loud and clear. For example, it was a grade in French that kept one of my sons off the honor roll. I was surprised because I had overheard him downstairs in the kitchen, tape recording himself to practice his pronunciation. When I asked his French teacher at a Home and School meeting to justify her low grade, she could produce no low test scores. Also, I asked why, if he had failed a test, it had not been sent home for my signature. No progress report had ever been sent home. She apologized and said it wouldn't happen again, but what if I had not spoken to her? On all subsequent report cards, my son made the honor roll.

A close friend of mine was speaking to the guidance counselor about her son attending one of the colleges of his choice. She was told that he would not be happy if accepted at any of the schools to which he had applied. "But," said my friend to the counselor, "You have not even asked my son's name yet." Fortunately, he was accepted at all the schools to which he applied, and made the Dean's List all four years.

It became necessary to give some thought to removing my children from the Boston schools. After my older son stated that he felt he was not being taught, I transferred him out of the system. There were many better-performing schools within the system; however, none were within our district. I knew of one such school I wished for my youngest to attend. I knew it would be difficult to get a transfer approved, but made the request nonetheless. As a parent very much involved in the Home and School Association (even through my years as a working mother, I never missed a meeting), I felt the need to press on to make this happen. I am happy to say that I was able to see this request come to fruition.

The efforts my friends and I put forth certainly paid off, and we are able to enjoy the success achieved by our children. My two sons were able to attain a higher education and are now working in the areas of behavioral science and mediation. And incidentally, my friend's son is now a teacher in the Boston public school system.

# THE BLACK PANTHERS

## *Cheryl Jackson*

I REMEMBER ARRIVING in Boston in the summer of 1967. I came in to the Trailways bus station when it was across from Boston Common. Greyhound was on the opposite side, and the Playboy Club was across the street.

At first, I felt a mixture of fear, excitement, and adventure. Because I was coming from a small town, I thought Boston was huge, with all the nightclubs, many stores, and the many choices for higher education, which brings me to my first job. Through a work-study program, I got my certificate from Copley's Secretarial School while working for the M.C.A.D./Jobs in Transportation, where I was transferred to Texaco's regional office in Chestnut Hill. I must say, this is the first time I actually encountered discrimination on the job.

While working for the Massachusetts Commission Against Discrimination, I found out that there were a lot of companies that were not hiring blacks. Texaco was one of them. When I was transferred there, I discovered that out of over fifty employees in the typing pool, I was the only black and the rest were white with the exception of one woman who was Jewish. This was, to say the least, a very uneasy experience. I say uneasy because of the times.

At this time, I was involved with the Black Panthers movement for what it originally stood for. Although it was thought that the Panthers were very militant, the organization was designed to open doors for the black brothers and sisters. They helped in educating the young and starting free meals in our school system and free meals on wheels for the elderly and disabled. The Black Panthers were trying to bring about self-esteem, black awareness, and bring the communities together making sure we could follow the words of James Brown: "Say it loud, I'm Black and I'm proud."

I really enjoyed being a part of this organization because it made me aware of my strengths and unafraid to compete in society. I must say it was exciting to meet leaders such as Stokely Carmichael, H. Rap Brown, Eldridge Cleaver, Nikki Giovanni, Angela Davis, Malcolm X, the Rev. Dr. Martin Luther King, and a host of others that in their own way contributed to the Black movement.

Another memorable feeling is the unity and love that I was shown as a member. There was always a feeling of self-worth. I remember one incident while attending one of our meetings on Blue Hill Avenue, where the headquarters was located. A young man came into the office quite distraught. One of the Brothers confronted him and asked what had happened. Instantly, a meeting was formed and we all became involved to support him. He was employed at Gillette in South Boston, and because of racism he had been terminated.

Finding children left out in the street unguarded was not acceptable to us. We would go to the children's homes and talk to the parents. We wanted to know what was going on so that we could help with the situation. The true Panthers cared. We were not militant; however, we were not afraid. We were not afraid of challenges because we met them too many times

before, and at times, much more harshly than you can imagine. We were determined resigned that our children would never have to face this.

It saddens me to look around today and see that after all the trials and tribulations that our fathers and forefathers have struggled and died for, we are still in the same dilemma that we have fought against and are still struggling. Why? We have earned the right to achieve. We must use it. First and foremost, we must utilize our education and skills. We are not the low man on the totem pole any more. We are intelligent, respectable, and educated human beings.

I am surprised and disappointed that we, the Panthers, were miscon-strued in our efforts to have unity in our community. In essence, I would like to say that I am truly thankful for my experiences growing up. I've witnessed a lot of good, some great, and, most of all, beautiful. I try not to think about the sad and sorrowful. I've survived them and that has made me strong.

Let it be known that we can always succeed if we allow ourselves to do so.

Be Blessed and Peaceful.

# REFLECTIONS ON CIVIL RIGHTS

*Daisy Janey*

IT WAS ALMOST forty years ago that my husband and I boarded a Greyhound bus and headed to the Black Power Conference in Newark, New Jersey, which lasted from July 20 to July 23, 1967. I invite you to reflect with me on the changes, individual accomplishments, and progress made since then.

The year 1967 was the culmination of what had been a tumultuous decade for America, with frustration over inequality erupting into riots across the country. In New Jersey, we saw the devastation first-hand. My husband and I were driven through the area by a conference member who was on the scene during the Newark revolt earlier that year. We saw block after block of destruction, iron grills torn out by bare hands frustrated by four hundred years of violence and oppression heaped on blacks. We saw windows marked "Soul Brother" peppered with police bullets. We saw the housing project where the mother of eleven was shot as she watched TV, shot because the police sprayed the building in search of an unseen sniper. She joins the long list of casualties of the Black revolution.

The conference itself came about through a meeting between Stokely Carmichael and Congressman Adam Clayton Powell in 1966. Under the chairmanship of Dr. Nathan Wright, author of *Black Power and Urban Unrest*, 192 organizations from thirty-six states and Bermuda convened to explore their areas of agreement and to develop an organizational and technical plan for the empowerment of black people.

In its July 21, 2003, issue, *Jet* magazine characterized the conference as the largest and most diverse group of American black leaders ever assembled.

The conference broke up into sixteen workshops ranging in content from black political, economic, civic, and educational power to social change, youth development, and the black woman. I entered the workshop on the black woman, facilitated by a very young and handsome Tony Brown. Security was tight, credentials were required for admittance, and then the doors were locked. You may be surprised to learn that we as black women were urged to allow black men to assume a dominant role in the black household. It cited the dangers inherent in a matriarchal society and stressed the difficulties the black woman would encounter in trying to throw off a role relegated to her by a slave society.

We returned to the general meeting with no resolution to offer but learned of one humorous incident. White reporters were barred from the conference. During a press conference in a neighboring church hall, white reporters were rousted by a group of youthful zealots. In fear of violence, reporters, photographers, and conference members alike made a hasty retreat through doors, windows, and whatever exit was available. In the melee, one conference member found herself greeting an old friend from behind the safety of a tombstone in a cemetery in the rear of the building.

*Dr. Martin Luther King, Jr., with Dr. Michael Haynes, and Daniel Janey.*
*This was taken during the civil rights march in Boston.*

## ROXBURY

More than twenty-five resolutions were adopted by the delegates including a call for the creation of black national holidays; a nationwide "buy black" effort; the establishment of black universities and a black speakers' bureau; cooperative buying of recording studios and radio and TV stations; condemnation of birth control as a plot to eliminate the black race; and support of Newark brothers in demanding release of those arrested in the Newark riot, including the dropping of all charges. Despite the great numbers of resolutions passed, only a few were actually implemented, among them a national holiday honoring Dr. King, the "buy black" effort, and eventually the Million Man March in Washington, D.C.

It's really amazing that so much has changed since 1967. Nationally, numerous cities large and small are headed by black mayors. Two African Americans have been elected governor of their states, most recently Deval Patrick here in Massachusetts. In the private sector, hundreds of blacks now hold top executive positions.

One huge change on a personal level involves my husband who, during World War II—wearing the uniform of the U.S. Armed Services —could not get a cup of coffee in Union Station (Washington, D.C.). Today, Union Station is staffed and directed by African Americans, and no one is denied service.

So we reflect on our progress and our missteps, and pledge our continual struggle for equal opportunity and justice for all.

# PART OF HISTORY

## *Dottie Pickup*

I WAS BORN IN SOUTH BOSTON many years ago. I lived on Marine Road near K Street, and my paternal grandparents lived on K Street near Marine Road, in the same house where my father grew up. Our back yards intersected. My grandfather died when I was very young, and after my grandmother died, we moved into the family home, where I lived until I got married. This house has been in our family since about 1890. One of my younger sisters still lives there.

When I was growing up, there were so many things for us to do: swimming lessons at the "L" (L Street Bathhouse) in the summer, ice skating in the winter at McNary (now Moakley) Park, school dances at the "Muni" (the South Boston Municipal Building, now the courthouse on East Broadway), roller skating at the rinks, and going to minstrel shows or the movies. I also played games like kick the can, dodgeball, and stickball with my siblings and the neighborhood kids. Some nights I would just sit on the doorstep learning to crochet from my mother. Those were the days when all the neighbors sat on the steps, especially on hot nights.

When I went to South Boston High School, I enjoyed walking to school with friends, hearing the latest gossip. Our teachers were friendly and

taught us a lot. Afternoons and during the summer, I worked in a Woolworth store on West Broadway. I worked the lunch counter with my girlfriend, "Sis," and we spent many summer days serving cold drinks and ice cream sundaes. The counter had twenty-six seats, so we each had thirteen to cover on Friday and Saturday nights after the regular girls left for the day. The many stores on West Broadway were open till nine o'clock on both nights. By the end of the day we were all covered in hot fudge and strawberry sauce, and very tired—until we heard that there was a dance somewhere! These were usually held at the Perkins Post at Fourth and O streets or at Hibernian Hall on Dudley Street. We both loved to dance, and someone from the band would let us know where they were playing.

After graduating from South Boston High, Class of 1946, I worked as a bookkeeper in a furniture store. In those days you didn't need a college education to get a good job when you graduated. I got married and raised seven children, four boys and three girls. I now have seventeen grandchildren and two great-grandsons! Most of my family still call Southie their hometown.

My husband, Ray, a World War II veteran, first forged his papers and enlisted in the Army at seventeen, to join with two of his older brothers. Ray and I became active with the South Boston Allied War Veterans Council and the Saint Patrick's/Evacuation Day Parade when his friend Ed Connolly was elected the 1968 chief marshal. Ed was looking for help from his friends to organize the parade, so I became secretary to the chief marshal. After that I was secretary to many of the chief marshals.

One of my favorite memories from those years is the 1976 bicentennial reenactment of the evacuation of the British from Boston. I've been told that my maternal ancestors (the Fitch family, after which Fitchburg is named) came to America shortly after the *Mayflower,* and that some of

189

them fought in the Revolutionary War, so perhaps that is why this event had special meaning to me.

According to "A Short History of Fort Independence" by Albert A. Swanson (printed in the program for the commemoration of the two hundredth anniversary of this battle), "Colonial troops did not gain the castle [Fort Independence was known as Castle William then], but they did fortify the hills in Dorchester with the cannons brought from Fort Ticonderoga by General Knox and company. On March 5, 1776, General Howe ordered all provisions withdrawn and the evacuation of the British troops began. By the seventeenth of March, the British had boarded ships and moved beyond the castle into the outer harbor. On the twentieth, Captain John Montressor blew up Castle William. The British symbol was destroyed, and on March 27, 1776, the British sailed out of Boston Harbor for Halifax, never to return."

The reenactment in 1976 took place on March 13 at noon in Marine Park. Those of us on the organizing committee all dressed in period costumes, and each of the sixty reenactment participants had a special part to play. Some played the British, others played colonists, including George Washington, Brigadeer General John Thomas, and Colonel Henry Knox. The "colonists" bombarded the fort at Castle William with make-believe cannons, and in response, people inside the fort set off fireworks to represent the explosions. The "British" surrendered, got in long boats at the lagoon, and rowed away. Then the grand Union flag was raised at the fort.

For nearly two hundred years after the evacuation of Boston by the British, the fort at Castle Island still plays a part in the defense of our country. During World War II, my uncle and his fellow soldiers were shipped off to war from Castle Island. Today it's owned by the Metropolitan District

Committee (MDC) and although it's no longer a military installation, it's a popular harbor park and recreation site.

After the reenactment, all the participants gathered at Farragut Statue and paraded over East Broadway to G Street to Dorchester Heights for the closing ceremonies. The Lexington Fife and Drum Corps provided the music. The honorable Judge Joseph Feeney was the narrator for the ceremonies at Dorchester Heights. The bicentennial torch was passed to Boy Scout Troup 268, South Boston, by Troop 66, Cambridge. Also speaking at the ceremonies were retired congressman John W. McCormack and Congressman John "Joe" Moakley. The program ended with a benediction, a salute to the flag, the playing of "Taps," the placing of a wreath to commemorate the event, and more music by the Lexington Fife and Drum Corps. The bicentennial celebration was an inspirational and fun day for me, when I got to dress up and play a part in the reenactment of history!

COURTESY MASS MEMORIES ROAD SHOW

*1976 Bicentennial Reenactment of Evacuation Day*

# THE WAR EFFORT

## *Esther Williams*

IN 1939 AMERICA ENTERED World War II in Europe and Japan. The military drafted many of our young men who had worked in the defense plants. This created a manpower shortage. So the government trained our young women to work in those jobs. I was trained to make cannons in the Watertown Arsenal where I worked the night shift until the end of the war. I had to get my birth certificate, have my fingerprints taken, and sign the papers of allegation before I was hired.

During this war, we were all one big united family. Fighting for our country, everyone sacrificing and contributing to the war effort. I think nearly every family had someone in the Army, Navy, Marines, or Air Force. At the post office, people were lined up trying to get their boxes of gifts in the mail so they would get to their soldiers before Christmas.

Even the school children wanted to show their support for our servicemen. My little sister talked her third grade teacher into having everyone in the class write a letter to my fiancé who was in England. The teacher put them all in one big envelope and sent them for the children. Jimmy and his whole troop really enjoyed every one of them. They sent the class a nice thank-you note letting the children know how much they appreciated them.

That same class won an award for collecting the most scrap metal for the government.

Everyone cooperated. When the air raid alarm went off, all lights went out. Air raid wardens walked the street to see that they did. We had ration books for every member of the family so the scarce food was distributed fairly. There was a USO where soldiers stationed in the nearby Army camps went on their time off to enjoy an evening of dancing. Our young ladies danced and served them light refreshments.

After the war when our men came home, we all got married and settled down. My husband and I were no exception; we were married December 25, 1945, and spent the next several years raising a family, buying a home, and just living a normal life.

However, it was during this time that I had one of the most memorable experiences of my life. Someone told me about this great civil rights march on Washington that was happening in a couple of days. I wanted to go, to stand up and be counted.

I had been reading about and seeing pictures of people in the South being bitten by dogs, fire hoses turned on them, police beating them (women and children also). These protestors were putting their lives in jeopardy fighting for all our people's civil rights. Though I knew I couldn't go down South, this march would give me a chance to participate.

I made some inquiries but found out I couldn't get a seat on one of the buses. They were all filled. I called my mother and asked her if she knew of any buses that were going. She said she would check, and if she found any she would go with me.

From 1948 to 1951, my mother was the first woman president of an NAACP branch office. She knew that the office would find us a seat if one was available. They checked and found the only two seats available were on a school bus a group of college students had managed to get and we could have them if we wanted them. We were happy to get them. To this day, every time I see or hear that famous speech of Dr. King, I get a thrill all over again.

When my husband Jimmy had come home after the war, we became active in the American veterans association AMVETS. Through state and national conventions, we met all kinds of people. From the shared experience of living through the war together, citizens' feelings of national pride and unity persisted. Our next goal became the fight for equality for all people in our country. Just as our community had been united in the war, we were still united and fighting a war for our civil rights.

# What We've Lost

# PROGRESS

## *Patricia Beckles*

### *I. The Elevated Trains*

I AM SLEEPING and I feel warm and safe. I am in my father's arms, and I bury my nose deep into his shirt, and I can smell his own personal smell and I know nothing can harm me, when all of a sudden I hear this terrific shriek; it is ear piercing; it snaps my eyes open and for a few seconds I feel as if I am falling and my whole world has ended.

I cannot recall my first ride on the El, but ever since I can remember there has been this dark structure. It was as if God had permanently stretched his palm over the sun. These giant cars would go by periodically, and although the ground did not shake I could feel the vibration through my feet. The sound of the train racing by was so loud you had to shout to be heard, and even then sometimes you could scream at the top of your voice and still, no one could hear you. The tracks that appeared to be suspended in space seemed to stretch for miles. There were curves where the train tilted to one side and I always thought the train would tip over and fall to the ground. Going around these curves, the wheels would screech so loud like brakes grinding on metal and I always felt that a disaster was about to happen.

This structure was built in the 1920s, and all my life I heard they were going to tear it down. Finally in the eighties they did tear down the El, including the beautiful stations like Dudley, Northampton, and Dover. These magnificent stations with their high mansard copper roofs, sturdy wooden floors, and miles of curved wrought iron railings, were all torn down and thrown away.

In its place I can now see the sun shining down on Washington Street. I can see that it is truly a boulevard, with four lanes of traffic. Gone are the neighbors who used to socialize in the shelter of the El. Although God has now removed his palm from the sun, and I no longer fear the trains falling from the sky, some days I can still hear the roar of the trains and that shriek of the wheels in my head, and I do not like progress.

*II. My Park*

It was the most beautiful park in the world. I had never heard of Central Park, but even after I did I still thought my park was the best. When I was small it seemed huge! It had eight entrances and they all met in the middle. There was a circle in the center where concerts were sometimes held. Each of the paths was cement, great for walking, roller-skating, or riding a bike. Everyone used the park as a shortcut. You could see tired men and women on their way home from work, or kids walking to and from school cutting through. There were benches all along the way, and they were almost always full. The large houses nearby spewed people out into the park at all hours of the day and night. People were always sitting with their baby carriages or just talking while kids played on the grass. The boys played ball all over the park. The girls would wrap their arms around each other and stroll along the paths and look at the boys and giggle.

Life revolved around the park. In the summer there were always carts with horses attached selling all kinds of fruits and vegetables: tomatoes, bananas, grapes, and the strawberries that were always the sweetest. Sometimes someone would buy a watermelon and cut it open for everyone to have a slice. I remember the taste of that melon and how we would try to see who could spit the seeds the farthest. Our hands were always sticky after eating the melon so then we would look for an ice cart. People at that time would put cards in their windows with the size ice they wanted, and the iceman would chip off a piece and carry it up the stairs to the apartment. While he was gone, we kids would jump up on the cart and get pieces of ice to put in our mouths to cool off. We would also use the ice to wash our hands and rub it on our faces.

I remember eating ice cream while sitting on a bench and then running to the fountain at the corner of the park at Sterling and Westminster streets to drink. The water always seemed so cool. Even the dogs would drink from it.

The park was so alive in the summer, there was always something happening. I remember having picnics there with my parents and my cousins. On the Fourth of July my dad and his brothers would set off fireworks. They had them in these little dirty brown paper bags, and sparklers and all kinds of things that made loud noises came from those bags. It made me shiver with fear.

Some of the trees had a ditch around the base and I would walk around each tree on my way to and from school. It was like an adventure. I could pretend I was in the jungle and had only grass and nuts to eat. I would bring peanut butter-and-jelly sandwiches and warm Kool-Aid and imagine all sorts of things.

The park in the fall with the leaves falling all different colors was like a wonderland. The noise the leaves made as I walked though them was like no other noise. I made big piles of them and then fell in them and covered myself with them.

In the winter the trees all covered with snow would look like monsters, and I pretended I was in a frozen wonderland. As I look back now the park was the center of my universe, and when I think of it, it always brings a smile to my face.

That was Madison Park, but like everything else it had to surrender to progress. The park is gone now and in its place stands a housing development. They are pretty little houses with little plots of grass and a few trees around, but what I wouldn't give to be able to walk though my park just once more, and see those magnificent trees, smell those aromas, and hear the voices of old.

# THE NOT-SO-BAD
# TRAGEDY

## *Wilma Browne*

IT WAS JULY 5, 1999, when we learned that our grandchildren, four-year-old Sabrae, and nine-year-old Roger, with their mother, Lisa, had been involved in an automobile accident in Alabama coming from a family reunion. Tragically, our beautiful granddaughter did not survive. This was a very sad time (it was the second time we had lost a granddaughter). It brought back another time when I was a child and my little friend Peggy Searcy was killed by a horse at the corner of Shawmut Avenue and Vernon Street in Roxbury. The horse had been frightened and went wild trampling her and another girl Juanita. Juanita survived. In those days horses and wagons were a common sight on the streets and especially ours (Shawmut Avenue) because there was a horse stable on it. These were very tragic and sad memories.

Another memory that stays with me starts with the time I came home from school to find my mother not at home and the house locked. Thankfully, this memory did not turn out as tragic. My brothers usually came home from school after I did. My father, naturally, was at work but my mother was always home reading a book or writing letters to her family.

When I arrived and she wasn't there, my first thought was that she was up on Washington Street still shopping. Washington Street in Roxbury at that time was a large shopping area with department stores, large markets, and so forth. I pictured my mother with her hand on her hip talking with Mrs. Carter, Mrs. Bennett, Mrs. Peters, or another person from the neighborhood. Since most people still had iceboxes, they shopped every day, and Washington Street was a big meeting place.

After another half-hour passed and still she had not come, I started getting very worried. This had never happened before. Finally, Richard (Dickie) a friend and classmate of my brother Donald's at Boston Trade High School, came by to tell me my mother was at the hospital with my brother. He said Donald had an accident at school while cutting wood on the machine and he had cut his hand off. He told me they had picked the hand up and put it in a wastebasket and took it to the hospital with him. I got so weak and nervous picturing my brother with a big bloody bandage on the end of his arm instead of his hand. My brother, who liked to draw and play softball and basketball, was now lying in the hospital with his hand cut off. I started to cry and then Dickie said, "Well, I don't think it was his whole hand, maybe it was just his finger," which made it a little better, but I was still very upset.

Finally, my mother came home and told me what happened. It seems my brother was making this little table in his carpentry class and cut the tip of his finger off. After being told he had his hand cut off, then a finger, the tip of the finger didn't seem so bad, even though it was. I never have forgotten the feelings I experienced that day. On the other hand, Dickie, who I saw recently after many years didn't remember the incident at all. The table Donald was working on turned out to be nice and sturdy. He painted it a rich mahogany and trimmed it in gold. We still have it today after fifty-nine years.

I have a few tragic memories, but the incident with my brother turned out to be not so bad after all and it brought back happier times in my childhood. Whether it was watching my father mix up unmeasured ingredients in a big yellow stoneware bowl to make his famous muffins on Sunday mornings or tasting the delicious oyster stuffing he prepared with the Thanksgiving dinner, I shall never forget these times.

Going away to summer camp wasn't an option for me. However, there were other programs provided in the schoolyards and at churches. I also attended the Cooper Community Center and the Norfolk House as well as the Whittier Street Pool and Cabot Bathhouse. My brothers went to the Robert Gould Shaw House. There were plenty of places to go in Roxbury and many things to do. In the winter, going to the Carter playground on Columbus Avenue to ice skate was a lot of fun, too. At times we saw football or baseball games, also tennis matches were played.

I went to churches of different denominations with my mother, but mostly we attended People's Baptist, Metropolitan, or Twelfth Baptist. We also went to various concerts and plays and listened to lectures. The older I got the more I appreciated it.

A caring family, a close-knit neighborhood, and the opportunity to to be a part of so many different activities made my childhood a very happy one. I was blessed to have grown up in Roxbury at the time that I did. I learned many lifelong lessons and made many lifelong friends.

# THE MORGAN HORSE

## ONE FAMILY'S EXPERIENCE
## OF THE DEPRESSION, 1926–1929

### *Mary Dorion*

MY FATHER DIED when I was three and in November 1924 my mother remarried. My stepfather, Edward Wilhelm was a handsome, blue-eyed man about five foot eight and well tanned. He had a pleasant singing voice and I recall sitting in his lap with my brother Joe rocking in my grandmother's oak rocker while he sang a song that had the words, "You can't play in my yard, you can't slide down my cellar door . . . if you won't be nice to me."

In the spring of 1924, Eddie and Mama bought a large house at 99 Baxter Street, with plenty of room at the side to keep his Model A Ford touring car, and at the back for children to play. Inside there was room enough for his new ready-made family and for his widowed mother.

Eddie had his own business as a produce dealer (peddler as they were called) that he had inherited from his father, a German immigrant. He delivered to small grocery stores and restaurants, and had a regular route selling to housewives in Dorchester and South Boston. I was very young but I do remember the talks after dinner, when Mama and Eddie counted up the day's receipts and decided what he needed for the market the next day. I remember the concern and worry about his customers who were running up bills they couldn't pay. Gradually, the business went down until he had to make a choice between paying the stable bills for his horse, Tom, or having enough money to go to the market to buy produce to sell the next day.

Eventually he had to give the title for Tom and the wagon to the stable owner to satisfy the feed and stable bills. Tom was a thoroughbred blue-ribbon Morgan horse, a breed noted for the heavy loads they could pull. Eddie's father had bought him for his son shortly before his death, and Eddie considered him to be part of the family. However, the arrangement allowed Eddie to take the team out on a daily basis in exchange for work around the stable and a payment for feed.

Winter was coming on. During these months, Eddie customarily went out only on days when there was no ice or snow, and delivered only "keepers"—potatoes, onions, etc.—and bags of kindling and coal. On such a day, delivering a load of wood, he was pulled aside by a policeman who asked to search the wagon. Finding two bottles of bootleg whiskey under the driver's seat, the policeman escorted Eddie to the stable with the team, confiscating his peddler's and teamster's licenses.

My memory includes the quarrels that ensued, the "how could you" and "you must have known better" and "what are we going to do now?" Eddie went out every day to look for work, but there were thousands of men looking. Mama found part-time work with the telephone company as a kitchen worker in the employee cafeteria. This caused more quarrels, for Eddie did not want his wife to work. A man of his generation consid-

ered it a disgrace, a black mark on his manhood, a testimony that he did not have the ability to support his family. This disagreement was solved when the steam table at the cafeteria malfunctioned, and Mama was badly burned on both arms.

My brother Joe and I did not realize the seriousness of the situation, but we knew something was wrong. We were aware of the quarrels and harsh words, and we knew it had to do with Mama working and Eddie drinking. At some point the gas was turned off for non-payment, and we started using kerosene lamps for lighting. My grandparents moved from downstairs to the house next door and Grandma still came every day when Mama worked. The bank foreclosed, the water was turned off, and we had to move.

Eddie took Joe to visit Tom at the stables sometimes on Sundays for a while, but then the stable owner had to sell out. Business had been bad, and many peddlers went out of business; Tom was sold to a new owner.

From then on I recall a series of cold-water flats. We moved at least once a year, usually because my parents got behind on the rent, and my grandparents had to bail us out. Sometimes Eddie found work, and we could move to a better flat, one with a copper boiler holding water heated by a pipe built into the firebox of the stove, or a flat that had electric lights.

I heard more and more Depression stories about no work, and families breaking up and going to live with relatives.

I recall hearing about landlords allowing otherwise good tenants to stay in their apartments over the winter in spite of being behind on the rent because the pipes would freeze and burst in the empty unheated flats. Banks were foreclosing, but there were no buyers and banks were failing. The Federal National Bank on Broadway near Perkins Square failed, and both Aunt Mary and Grandma lost some of their savings.

Aunt Mary operated the small lunchroom at the Czech club next to her house and kept us going with day-old bread and other leftovers from which Mama, a creative cook, could make a hearty meal. In spite of growing up in a household of plenty, she had inherited skills handed down from generations of country people as practiced by Grandma — make it do, make it last, or make it over.

All kinds of strategies were practiced to stay afloat. Houses built before the twentieth century were drafty and uninsulated with windows that rattled and no central heat. To conserve heat, all doors leading off the kitchen were closed. Bedroom doors were opened about an hour before bedtime to allow a little heat in. Sidewalk bricks or flatirons were heated in the oven and wrapped in towels to put at the foot of the bed. Rugs were rolled and placed against the outside doors to stop the drafts.

Nothing was wasted. Grandma saved the string with which most parcels were tied (before Scotch tape). She rolled it into balls according to thickness and used it to crochet hot plate mats. She taught me how to make cat's tail cord using a thread spool with small brads nailed in the top, with her balls of string. Then she made chair pads from the cording. We saved paper. Tissue paper was a substitute for the toilet roll, as was crumpled newspaper if nothing else was available. Brown paper was used to drain bacon, fried potatoes, fish cakes, etc., and the cooking grease became laundry soap.

Mama was a skilled seamstress and had always made our clothes, but now she made over discarded items, and if she absolutely had to buy something, Filene's Basement was the place to go. In those days you could buy a pair of kids' shoes for as little as twenty-five cents.

Food was the big problem. Trying to keep the family fed for next to nothing was the challenge. Breakfast was oatmeal with evaporated milk cut half-and-half with water. To drink, we had cocoa with evaporated milk. Toast was made on top of the stove and spread with oleomargarine. Margarine was in its infancy then, consisting of a one-pound block of lard and a small packet of powdered carotene. To use it, the housewife worked the block until it was softened, sprinkled the orange powder over the top, and then kneaded the whole until it was a uniform color. *Voila!* Ersatz butter.

Lunch might be a cheese or peanut butter sandwich or a ketchup sandwich. To satisfy the sweet tooth, bread and butter was sprinkled with sugar. In winter it was soup for lunch. During cold weather there was always a fire in the stove, and Mama had a pot going all the time with water drained from vegetables, soaking yellow peas and ham bones, or whatever scraps she thought would make a good soup. As I recall, the only thing my mother cooked that I couldn't swallow was kidney stew.

Mama had a rule that we couldn't leave the table until we had finished everything on our plates. On kidney stew night I sat and sat while the kidney stew got colder and more unpalatable. We always had a cat, and I surreptitiously fed the meat to the cat while I forced the broth and vegetables down. Strangely, fifty years later I remember sitting in the National Museum restaurant in Dublin savoring a plate of kidney stew soup and wishing I had the recipe.

In 1926, Eddie was admitted to the tuberculosis sanitarium, and Mama became eligible for public assistance. Although the amount was small it was enough to rent a decent flat with electricity and hot water. Mama's pride and self-respect were constantly battered through all of this. She cried a lot, especially after my sister Helen became ill. Helen had caught cold and was sent to what was called a fresh air camp for frail children, where she stayed for six months.

In early spring 1929, Eddie died. Since we had no telephone, a policeman came with the news. I was in the kitchen when Mama came to tell me. I recall that she was very pale, and she started to cry. I don't recall feeling any emotion, not even sorrow. In retrospect, it had been little more than four years since our family started on this downhill slide, having reached bottom when Eddie was diagnosed with tuberculosis. It was fixed in my eight-year-old mind through all the quarrels, abuse, and cruel recriminations, that Eddie was the cause of it all — the fear, worry, and privation. I didn't understand Mama's sorrow. Strangely I did understand her distress when she said, "How am I going to tell his mother?"

Later Helen came home chubby and healthy with rosy cheeks and my mother seemed to recover her equilibrium. I started sixth grade at the Gaston School. In October the papers were full of headlines about the stock market crash and suddenly everyone was reading about the Depression that we had been living through for the past five years.

# UNCLE JOE

## *Mary Kane*

ON A NICE DAY in 1946, my family went down to meet a ship
bringing home soldiers who served overseas in World War II.
These soldiers had been in the Battle of the Bulge before being captured by the Germans. This was the first time I saw my uncle Joe.
He was my mother's half brother and my mother was close to him. Joe
was a big man physically. He was five foot eleven, with light brown hair
in crew cut, but when he came off the ship he was very thin and sick. All
around us, soldiers were taking the hands of their children. Joe took my
hand, like a father would, and we were together every day after that. We
went everywhere together. I was eight years old.

At home, life was busy. My father was in and out of our lives because of
his drinking. We lived on the corner of F and Second Streets. There was
a small store nearby and over this store lived my maternal grandmother
and my two uncles.

Our house had four rooms with the toilet in the hall. My two brothers
and I slept in the back bedroom. My brothers had bunk beds and I had a
small bed. My parents had a bedroom between the kitchen and parlor. In
the kitchen was a large, cast-iron wood and coal stove. The large black

sink was by the front door. We had to heat water as it was a cold-water flat. In the winter there was always a kettle with hot water and a line on the back of the stove where we dried our socks and mittens. When we came in we took our boots off and sat in front of the oven with our feet there to warm them.

After my uncle came home, he spent some time in the hospital because he was so sick. Even when he was released, he had seizures during which he would tremble and foam at the mouth and then black out. I used to stay with him to make sure he didn't hurt himself. I found out later that he had been castrated without anesthesia while he was a prisoner of war. He had multiple infections, and had been kept at a hospital for several months before he was sent home to us. He also had tuberculosis. As time went on, he got a little better and we used to go for walks up Broadway toward East Broadway to the beach and back. Sometimes we would go to the beach for the whole day, and sometimes he took me to the aquarium to see the seals and fish.

We spent a lot of time together and he was more of a father to me than my own father. He talked sometimes about the war and the things he had to do, and how he felt about his time in the service. He told me how they had to bomb a village so the Germans couldn't use it to hide and kill American soldiers. He felt bad because they were people's homes, and because some of the villagers refused to leave before the bombing began; they said they had nowhere else to go. He told me how he was captured. He was driving at night on the side of a mountain and didn't have the headlights on. They were supposed to take a sharp curve and missed it, and went over the side of the road. They were captured by German soldiers after they crashed. He was a prisoner for I don't know how long. He saw a lot of destruction and felt bad for the people. He used to talk about how these things made life hard for the children, especially those who lost parents. He was also there with Patton when they went into the death camps and saw the ovens and the prisoners. These things he never forgot but rarely mentioned.

Uncle Joe liked books and magazines. Sometimes I would read to him and then we would talk about the books afterward. On Sunday nights, he turned off all the lights in the house and we listened to the radio, shows like *The Shadow* and *Inner Sanctum*. He was very easygoing and liked practical jokes. He liked to go over to the corner tavern with the guys. Sometimes if he was in pain, he'd have a couple of drinks; otherwise, he was not much of a drinker. He was easy to talk to and liked telling jokes or playing pranks. He didn't like fighting or people who were hard to get along with.

Over time, he stopped going out because he was feeling sick again and he was depressed. He had been seeing a girl he hoped to marry, but he also knew that he couldn't have children. He didn't feel like a man anymore. Then she stopped coming to see him. Eventually, he knew that she had met someone else, and I think he was happy for her. He saw everything from his window, the kids playing and the people coming and going from the neighborhood. Some people used to stop under his window to talk to him.

He was getting sicker but refused any help. Once when Joe learned that the doctor wsa coming to visit, he pulled himself together and tried to look healthy so that the doctor would go away.

Then he got very sick and was bedridden. He was thin and weak, and ate very little. He coughed and lost the use of his legs and lower body. After everything that he'd been through, he didn't want to live anymore and refused to see a doctor. I used to go out and give him supper and stay and read to him or just talk until my mother came out after feeding the younger kids at seven thirty or eight o'clock. I then went around the corner to our house and she would stay with him for a couple of hours. Then she would check on us and then go back until my grandmother came home from work around one or two o'clock in the morning. My grandmother worked in the Colonial Building cleaning the offices. (When my grandmother first came here from Galway, Ireland, she worked as a maid cleaning and ironing for people in Jamaica Plain.)

Uncle Joe died February 26, 1951, at home. At 7:25 P.M. that same night, my father came into our house and said, "Uncle Joe is gone." But I didn't understand that he was gone. I didn't realize that I would never see him again until I went to the funeral and heard them play "Taps." I was thirteen.

When we were driving home from the funeral I turned around in the seat to look back toward the cemetery, where he would always stay. I took his death very hard. In school, I sat in class and looked out at the flag. There was a giant flagpole across town at Mount Holyoke Cemetery that I could see from my classroom. In my mind, that flag represented his burial spot. I couldn't concentrate at school and refused to speak in class. I felt my body shutting down; I didn't care about anything. Nothing mattered anymore. Our doctor told my mother I had a complete breakdown. Actually, I didn't talk for about two years. My mother sent me to live with my grandmother, who had just moved to the D Street projects, which had been veterans housing. Mothers of veterans could live there, and she moved in.

At first I didn't care where I lived because I was grieving for my uncle. Then as time went on I enjoyed it. She taught me to crochet and knit and to iron like she did, and to make soup with all kinds of veggies cut big so you saw and knew what you were eating. On Sundays we listened to Christian shows on the radio. On Saturdays we went food shopping, sometimes to Blackstone market, which is now called Haymarket.

As time passed, I got better and went back home and went to school and graduated.

As an adult I look back to things I learned from my uncle and what he told me about the war and other things. I remember he was always watching me to see how I behaved. One day he got very mad at me. The neighbors across the street from us had come from Germany. They had four kids, who still spoke with German accents. Some other kids had them cornered and were throwing rocks at them. I was sitting on a fire hydrant, watching, but I didn't say anything.

My uncle called me upstairs and was angry. I said I wasn't doing anything. He said, "You were sitting, watching, and by doing this, you were giving permission." He told me how much of their country had been destroyed by war. He knew what they must have gone through before moving here. As a child I didn't understand, but I tried to be friendly to the children afterward. I even did a book report on Germany for school, because no one else wanted to learn anything about that country in the years after the war. Then I learned about all the destruction there and the culture of the people who lived there. When those German kids came to live in South Boston, they had to learn a new way of life and some people were cruel to them. So were some kids after they heard what their parents said about the Germans. But I also learned that their grandparents had been killed in a raid in Germany.

As an adult, I saw firsthand what my uncle Joe meant when one of my coworkers was treated unfairly by other coworkers. They tried to get me to go along and I refused and because I kept refusing they finally stopped and allowed her to be part of the celebration they had tried to stop her from joining. This is how I will always remember my uncle Joe. He taught me kindness.

# CHANGES IN
# THE NEIGHBORHOOD

## *Mattie Powell*

T HE FRESH vegetable and fruit stands on the avenue have vanished. It was my pleasure to walk and shop knowing that whatever I bought was fresh. Sometimes I would call in my order on the phone. Now I have to drive to the Stop & Shop or other supermarket. I find water being sprinkled on the vegetables to keep them alive, as they have traveled miles packed in huge dark trucks. The fruits are crowded into big net bags and have endured bruises from being handled by many hands.

I miss the smell of freshly baked bread. The bakeries are nonexistent. While out shopping I was sure to stop at the bakery. Freshly baked cakes, cookies, and pies lined the showcase. I would choose a big loaf of bread and have it sliced. These too are now on the shelves of the big stores. My corner grocery store where I would pick up a few things and be on my way is gone. Now I stand in a long line anxiously waiting at the cash register of some supermarket.

It pains me to mention the butcher shops that have disappeared. "Good morning, Mrs. Powell. What can I do for you today?" the butcher, in starched-white apron and hat, would say cheerfully, smiling to show he was glad I came. I would order a big roast beef that he cut before my eyes. Then lamb chops trimmed and cut. If I wanted hamburger it was cut and put into the grinder. The meat stand now at the supermarket holds all these in compartments including chickens and turkeys. Legs go with legs, wings with wings in plastic trays covered with plastic. The skinned breasts are undesirable to look at, but they are helpful for weight control.

The store I really grieve for is my corner drugstore. I woke up one morning and found it gone without word or even a hint that it was leaving. I would fill my prescriptions immediately or ask advice from the pharmacist on duty. I could send my children there without fear of them running into undesirables.

A special treat after going to a movie in my neighborhood was a serving of ice cream at the drugstore. Huge dips of colorful ice cream came from the big pails. My favorite — a banana split — was a real treat. I loved to watch the owner make milk shakes and sundaes. The kids loved sitting at the counter turning on stools — one look from me stopped that activity right away. The people were polite; there was no swearing or loud talking. Children or adults enjoyed themselves immensely. The store stayed open until eleven o'clock.

Now it is a different story. Liquor bottles are lined up side by side against the walls. Customers are swearing, some staggering, asking for anything that will dull their senses and take them from reality. Drug dealers stand outside on the corner, waiting to strike a deal. One is afraid of drive-by shootings, a bag being snatched, or hearing swear words by the dozens. It is fearful to be out at night. Early morning before the liquor store is opened winos are lined up counting their change in order to buy a bit of wine.

As my community continues to change I am happy to witness again some positive aspects. Thanks to Mayor Menino, formerly boarded-up buildings and vacant lots are now crowned with affordable housing. Handsome bright-colored swings, slides, and jungle bars are standing on playgrounds in parks ready for children to play. After-school programs are established to help with homework in every community. Flowers of beautiful hues and fragrances greet us on every corner throughout the city. I have an open letter to the mayor written in 2003 thanking him for the flowers.

The sad part is that crime is still rampant in my community. Families cannot relax and enjoy themselves for fear of the violence and shootings. Young black teenagers are killing each other and innocent children as well. Prayer is very much needed today and a plan to make Sunday school a compulsory part of education. But as the community changes from time to time, I am certain that "this too shall pass."

# MY NEIGHBORHOOD

## *Rose Toscano*

O N SEPTEMBER 27, 1927, I came from Italy, at the age of two, with my mother and father. We came from Nicastro, Calabria, in the southern part of Italy to stay with my Uncle Pat in the North End until we found an apartment. Our first apartment was two large rooms on Harris Street (off of Hanover Street) in a wood-shingled three-story house. These were cold-water flats, heated by wood and coal in large black potbellied stoves. The lights were gas, and we kept our food in iceboxes.

The neighbors were mostly Italian and Irish with Jewish merchants (who spoke Italian). Many of the stores had credit by the week. Where restaurants now line Salem Street, there were "mom-and-pop" stores for clothing, shoes, hardware, and groceries; bakeries, a five-and-dime, several small hotels, and more than one Chinese laundry. There was an open-air market for fruit and vegetables — not Haymarket, but right on Salem Street — with carts and vendors.

We did not have lots of money, but there was lots of love and kindness for others: helping sick neighbors, helping with small children, sharing food and clothing if needed. We grew up in a very happy atmosphere.

Radios and Victrola were our only entertainment. After dinner, neighbors came over to listen. My mother would place a large quilt on the kitchen floor, and we children would lie down and listen to music or the dramas on *Lux Theater* or a mystery called *The Shadow*. My mother would serve hot cocoa and biscuits.

During the summer my mother would take us to the North End Beach (where the pool is now) from ten o'clock in the morning to three in the afternoon. Originally, the coast guard wanted the area for a marina, but residents here marched on city hall in protest. The smooth sand was trucked in and the water was so clear that at high tide, when the water covered the thirty or forty steps down to the beach, you could see every one. There was a nice bathhouse on one side with showers and changing rooms. You could even rent bathing suits there (made of cotton in those days). People would sit and sun themselves on the benches on the piers, and the kids would dive off the piers and swim the long distance to the Navy yard, their mothers screaming after them. I was too scared to go that far. Everyone packed a lunch, and there was one variety store across the street that sold soft-serve ice cream. Now, near the pool, there is a concession stand that sells hot dogs, candy, and ice cream.

After school, we had many programs, including dramatics, sewing, knitting, and painting. We kids had three places to go: the North Bennett Street School, the Catherine Moore House on Tileston Street, and the North End Union on Parmenter Street.

The North Bennett Street School had a big room where kids could drop in after school and play games and socialize. We were disappointed that the City didn't help the neighborhood keep this as a community center; it has now been taken over by the North Bennett Street School.

The Catherine Moore House was run by nuns of Saint Joseph. There was a rooftop playground — enclosed of course — with swings, seesaws, etc. On the street level there was a gym with a basketball court. That building has been taken over by Sacred Heart Church, and houses families from overseas who have children in the hospital and need a place to stay.

The North End Union was originally a settlement house, built to help the people. There, we had plays, cooking classes, and fundraisers. One such fund raiser was a weekly ten-dollar meal for which different restaurants would donate food (at which Barbara Maldero and I were asked to serve). This building was sold to a developer who wanted to turn it into condos, but it now stands empty as they negotiate zoning laws. (The Christopher Columbus School was also sold for condos and their gym on Prince Street, which was bought by the archdiocese and became the Saint Leonard's Community Center, was then sold for six million dollars and is now condos too, as is the old Seaman's House.)

One other place we went after school was the library. The North End used to have a beautiful library on North Bennett Street (not the small one we have today), with marble statues and a circular staircase as grand as the Boston Public Library in Copley Square. We'd go there every day to do our homework at the big round tables, in silence. The only communication was through passing notes. I guess the upkeep cost too much, and it was closed a long time ago.

In the evening the grownups would sit on the front steps and watch the children play while they mended, knitted, or socialized. Since there weren't as many cars then, we could play in the street. Our signal to go home was the street lamp coming on, unless our parents were still out. We played jump rope, hide-and-seek, hopscotch, jacks, marbles, and a game called relievio that was like red rover. I didn't play that much because the boys were too rough. Also in the evening, the schools and churches showed movies for five cents.

The only building now still functioning as a community center is the Nazzaro Center on North Bennett Street. This building was the neighborhood public bathhouse (most of the apartments did not have showers or tubs in the thirties, forties, fifties, etc.), and is now used for after-school programs and senior meetings. The director there is very good with children, and the North End Against Drugs group has a variety of activities, programs, and trips for kids. I am the president of the North End Younger Seniors, one of the senior clubs that meets there to play bingo, have coffee, and socialize. Every year, the two age groups come together when the seniors buy tickets for the North End Against Drugs banquet and fundraiser. At the banquet, trophies and awards are given out for sports, community service, etc. So even without all the community centers we used to have, the North End still holds true to its community values.

The North End Christmas Fund Luncheon was begun twenty years ago by Fred Carangelo. Despite being wheelchair-bound due to muscular dystrophy, Fred is constantly working on programs for the neighborhood. He thought the Christmas Fund would be a good thing for the elderly who were homebound, to cheer them up at Christmas. At first the Fund provided nightgowns and pajamas, then a pound of coffee and a check, and now just a larger check. They are given not only to the homebound, but to anyone who may be lonely or had a difficult year. The Luncheon raises the funds for these gifts. It is held at Tecce's Restaurant, which donates the food. Bakeries also donate pastries, and the tickets cost fifteen dollars. There is also a raffle to raise money. In this and many other ways, our community spirit is very much alive in the North End.

# About the Authors

WILMA BROWNE was born in Roxbury in 1935, the youngest and only girl with three brothers. She was educated by the Boston public school system and retired from the U. S. Postal Service in 1992. She and her husband Ralph have been married fifty-six years and have seven children, eleven grandchildren, and five great-grandchildren.

PATRICIA BECKLES was born in Boston on June 5, 1933, and was educated in the Boston schools. She graduated from Girls' High School in 1950 and is one of five first cousins to graduate from the Massachusetts Memorial Hospital School of Nursing. She recently had an article published in the Alumnae Association Bulletin on the fiftieth anniversary of her graduation from nursing school. She has been married to her loving husband Orman for fifty-two years, has one son, one granddaughter, and three great-grandchildren. She says, "Yes, the neighborhoods have changed, but being surrounded by many cousins and lifelong friends has kept the memories fresh." She is an avid reader and has always wanted to write.

MARY E. CLARKE was born in Ohio and had five sisters and two brothers. Her father was a minister and her mother stayed at home. A community activist all of her adult life, Mary lived and worked in Columbia Point as a Head Start teacher for twenty years. She retired from Head Start as a supervisor in Dorchester after thirty years. She was president of the Columbia Point Health Center, the first non-profit community health center in the United States, where she also served as its vice president and treasurer. She took courses in early childhood education at Wheelock College. The mother of eight children (four boys and four girls), Mary now has fourteen grandchildren and six great-grandchildren. She works part-time at the Hildebrand Family Shelter in Cambridge, where she emphasizes the importance of education. "I've always enjoyed giving back to the community and supporting others."

ANGIE DEMINICO was born and raised in Boston's North End in 1940. She was the youngest of four children. "I would not trade being born and raised in the North End at that time, even with all the technology and advancement today."

ANN E. DESILVA was born in South Boston and has spent her life there. She attended South Boston High School, and worked for the federal government for thirty-two years. She has a great daughter plus two wonderful grandchildren. Her interests are music, the Senior Center, and the South Boston Yacht Club. She loves living near the ocean and helping others.

MARY AGNES DONOVAN was Georgia-born, Florida-raised, and now makes her home in South Boston. She was married for twenty years and had seven children. "I can't think of any other place I would like to live. Here I have my beloved Atlantic Ocean, sailing, walks along the beach, and a thirty-five-minute walk to downtown Boston. I have everything I want and everything I need. I have four seasons to keep watch for — the most spectacular is autumn's changing colors, when God unleashes a painter's palette."

MARY DORION was born on November 9, 1919, in South Boston, one of three children. She was educated in the Boston school system and graduated from South Boston High. Mary married a local boy, Frank Dorion, and had four children. After her children were grown, she returned to school to earn a B.S. in Education, majoring in learning disabilities, and now uses her talents as a literacy volunteer with several agencies in the Boston area.

PEG FAHEY is the seventh daughter of her parents' eight children. She was born in South Boston and raised in Dorchester, where she lived for forty years in a twelve-room home. She graduated from J.E. Burke High School in 1954, took night classes at Boston University, and attended Babson Institute. She worked in various executive secretary positions for forty-five years.

JENNA (COAKLEY) FITZGERALD, a South Boston native who still resides in South Boston, married Gerard Fitzgerald, a Boston school custodian. They followed the American dream and had six beautiful children, all of whom received college educations. Jenna worked as a paraprofessional in Boston public schools. She then joined her kids in college and moved on to become a Boston Teacher Union field representative, recently having won the prestigious Albert Shanker Pioneer Award from the American Federation of Teachers in Washington, D.C.

PEG FOLEY is eighty years young and was born and brought up in the Cathedral Parish of the South End of Boston. She was the youngest of four children. She's of Scotch-Canadian descent and both of her parents were from Prince Edward Island, Canada. She graduated from Girls' High School in 1944 and went to work for the Western Union during World War II. She retired from the South Boston Library seventeen years ago. She's the mother of five children, seven grandchildren, and one great-grandson. She keeps active as much as possible with exercise, line dancing, and attending the Senior Center. She's married to a retired Boston firefighter and lives at City Point in a top-floor apartment with a beautiful view of the downtown area.

MARY FRASCA was born in the North End. She worked for the Italian newspaper *La Gazzetta del Massachusetts* for over twenty years while raising her two sons, Richard and Robert. She also worked as a legal supervisor at Continental Insurance Company and as an administrator at the North End Union. She is currently a paralegal at Greater Boston Legal Services.

ANTHONY FRISSORA, born in 1925 in Watertown, Mass., grew up in a family of thirteen surviving children. He attended grammar and high schools in Watertown, and later enlisted in the U.S. Navy during World War II, and graduated from Wentworth Technological Institute. In 1985, he retired as a mechanical engineer from Allied-Signal. Anthony and his wife Sona have been married for fifty-two years.

SONA FRISSORA was born in Dorchester, Mass. She graduated from Albertus Magnus College in New Haven, Conn., and also attended Boston University. Sona worked for AT&T and, before retiring ten years ago, was the Director of Education for the Morris County Board of Realtors in New Jersey. Married fifty-two years, Sona and her husband Anthony have four sons and nine grandchildren. They settled in the North End ten years ago and couldn't be happier.

KEITHA B. HASSELL was born and raised in Roxbury. She taught school in Plymouth, Mass.; Syracuse, N.Y.; and Boston. She retired from the David A. Eliss School, incidentally the same school she attended as a kindergartener. Keitha has one sister and is the mother of four adult children and the grandmother of three.

VIRGINIA FITZGERALD HAYES, "Nina," is a fourth generation South Bostonian. Twelve years of parochial school education taught by nuns and strict Catholic parents shaped her early years. College, Vietnam, marriage, and parenthood changed her perspective as a young adult. Nina was awarded a B.A. with honors in psychology ten days after her third child was born. She taught at South Boston High and Cardinal Cushing High for many years before returning to the University of Massachusetts to earn a Master's degree from the McCormick Institute. The next ten years Nina was a registered lobbyist on Beacon Hill, and currently she is the Executive Director of the American Society of Interior Designers, New England Chapter. Nina lives in South Boston with her husband Richard; they have three grown children and a granddaughter, Maeve.

ALICE HODGE was born an only child in Cincinnati, Ohio, and moved to Boston in her early years. Alice was educated in the Boston public school system and attended the University of Massachusetts–Boston. She retired after twenty-six years dedicated to public service of the Commonwealth of Massachusetts, and remains very active in her community. She has been a den mother, leader of the Gladys R. Holmes unit of the Women's Missionary Society of the Charles Street AME Church, as well as a member of the Roxbury Senior Care Program and the Freedom House Goldenaires. In 2002, she received the annual African American Achievement Award from Mayor Menino. She is the proud parent of two sons, grandmother of three, and great-grandmother of four.

ANNA IRVING was born at home on June 20, 1932, on Columbus Avenue in Roxbury. She attended the Commins School on Mission Hill, the High School of Practical Arts, Massachusetts College of Art, and Boston Clerical School. She became a widow at age twenty-five and felt it necessary to occupy her time with learning. She attended the New England Institute of Banking and studied five computer languages as well as psychology, auditing, and law. "When I was about thirty-two, I remarried and found that I had picked a lemon in the garden of love." She has been a widow again now for twenty years. She retired after working in Boston banks for more than thirty years and took on several volunteer assignments, including treasurer of her alumni association, president of the Friends of the South Boston Branch Library, and tour guide at Fort Independence on Castle Island. She attended school until age sixty-two, though she hopes to take more classes soon at the University of Massachusetts. "My children now have their own lives and I am free!"

CHERYL JACKSON has lived in Boston for more than forty years. Currently she is in a training program sponsored by the Urban League of Eastern Massachusetts and plans to work for the City of Boston's Department of Elder Affairs. She has three children and nine grandchildren. In her spare time she crochets, reads, and loves to socialize. She strives to follow her mother Mabel Jackson's advice, "Good, better, best, never let it rest, until the good becomes the better and the better becomes your best."

DAISY JANEY was born in 1920, in St. Helena, a small island off the coast of Beaufort, South Carolina. She grew up in Everett, Mass., until moving to Washington, D.C., in 1941 for the duration of World War II. She is a widow with three children and three grandchildren. After many years of employment in non-profit agencies, she is retired and living in Hingham, Mass.

BEATRICE JONES lives in Hyde Park with her husband of fifty-five years, Joseph Jones, who is a retired postal worker and Navy man. They have three children, two grandchildren, and one great-grandchild. She is active in the YMCA's program Seniors On the Move, and Boston Public Health Commission's Reach 2010 Coalition. Beatrice is a Steward of the Grant AME Church. She enjoys cooking, tai chi, yoga, crocheting, reading, and traveling. She loves to be on the go. "Do the best that you can, trust in the Lord, and always try to help someone who is less fortunate than you are. Love is the best of all."

MARY KANE was born April 2, 1939, and has lived in South Boston all of her life. Her family was all from South Boston, and both sets of her grandparents came over from Ireland. Eight years ago she retired from Gillette after fifteen years in various positions including packer, machine operator, and security. She now visits the South Boston Senior Center, where she manages the kitchen two days a week, and also spends time making dolls, afghans, quilts, and altered books. She has a cat named Candy Kane and a new puppy named Sugar Kane.

BARBARA KNIGHT was born in 1935 in Burkeville, Virginia. She graduated from the Luther H. Foster High School in Hathoway County, Virginia, class of 1953. She moved to Boston in 1958 where she attended the University of Massachusetts for two years. She has always wanted to write and draw. Her life work is in human services, working with children and the homeless. She is a mother of seven biological children and five with whom she was blessed. She is a grandmother of twenty-one and a great-grandmother of fifteen.

MARION LECAIN was born in Boston and grew up in Arlington, Mass. She married in 1947 and had four children. In 1960, as a single parent, she bought a three-family house in Winthrop. She went back to work as a part-time bookkeeper for a travel company when her youngest went to school. In 1992, after more than thirty years in the travel industry, she retired. She attended Suffolk University in Boston and graduated with the class of 2000. She moved to South Boston in 2004 and loves it. "I live on the first floor of my daughter and son-in-law's house and don't need a car. I can walk a half a block to East Broadway and visit the library, the bank, Stop & Shop, or Brooks. I am very happy there!"

HELEN MCHUGH was born in South Boston on January 1, 1931. The eighth child born into a family of ten children, Helen is a graduate of St. Augustine's High School class of 1948 and one year at Boston Clerical Business School. After being a stay-at-home mother, Helen returned to work at Verizon and retired in 1996. Helen is married and the mother of three girls and six grand-children.

JOSEPH MCHUGH was born in a three-decker on West Third Street in South Boston in 1930. He is a graduate of South Boston High School. He served in the U.S Naval Construction Battalion on Kwajalien in the Marshall Islands in the early 1950s. Being a late bloomer, he received a four-year degree from the University of Massachusetts–Amherst in 1983. After toiling for thirty years, he retired from the Boston Edison Company in 1990. He is the father of eight children, grandfather of seventeen, and great-grandfather of one.

BARBARA MALDERO was born on November 1, 1927, as Barbara Santa Bruno in Boston's North End, where her family has lived for several genera-tions. "I can, therefore, be considered a true 'North Ender.'" She attended Cushman Public School, which is now the North End Public Library, then Hancock Public School, and Michelangelo Public School where she graduat-ed in 1943. Both Hancock and Michelangelo schools are now condominiums. She graduated from the High School of Practical Arts in 1946. In 1949, she married Louis Maldero at Saint Leonard of Port Maurice Church, where her parents were married in 1917. She has two children, Stephanie and Vito. Her husband passed away in 1977. She retired from Blue Cross Blue Shield. She is active in her community as vice president of the North End Younger Seniors, and on the boards of Villa Michelangelo Housing and the Nazzaro Center. She organized the Saint Damian Group, which makes a range of items to send to people in need.

RITA (PALERMO) MULKERN was born in the North End on December 16, 1929. Her father was born in Taurasi, Italy, and came to Boston at the age of nine. Her mother was a native North Ender, born on Moon Street: "She never left the North End and never wanted to." Rita attended Boston public schools—Eliot, Michelangelo, and Girls' High. Her father supported her decision to enroll at Northeastern University in 1948. In 1953, she graduated with a B.A., and in 1955, she obtained an Ed.M. That same year, she began her career as an elementary school teacher, retiring in 1993. She married professor John R. Mulkern on August 26, 1956. They have three children—Stephen, Michael, and Lauren—and all three graduated from Boston Latin. In 1996, she and John moved to North Square, where she had grown up, and many of her old friends from childhood still live nearby.

Dottie (Mascal) Pickup was born in the old Carney Hospital in South Boston, the second oldest of five daughters born to Robert and Florence (Fitch) Mascal. She attended Nazareth Grammar School and graduated from South Boston High School, class of 1946. Dottie married Raymond Pickup in 1951, and together they raised seven children: four boys and three girls. They have seventeen grandchildren and two great-grandsons. Dottie was the first female secretary in the South Boston Citizens' Association, has held various offices in the South Boston Residents' Group, assisted in writing the by-laws for the Castle Island Association, and volunteers for the Boys' State American Legion program.

Barbara Porter is the single parent of four adult children and six grandchildren. Following her retirement as a registered nurse at Boston City Hospital thirteen years ago, Barbara became heavily involved in community activism. She provided the community with health-related presentations and workshops, and served in volunteer capacities with several regional and national disease education, detection, and prevention health organizations. Barbara has received numerous awards and citations for her efforts. She resides in Mattapan and her hobbies include baking and gardening.

Mattie B. Nobles Powell was born in Rochester, New York, and educated in Aiken, South Carolina. She moved to Boston at an early age and was one of the first women to become a master barber. Mattie graduated from Boston State College with a Master's degree in early childhood education and taught kindergarten for many years in the Boston public school system. She enjoys writing poetry.

EILEEN MAY RICHARDSON was born in Boston and grew up in Roxbury in a little stone house with a backyard. She attended the Dillaway School, St. Joseph Grammar, and Girls' High School, and earned her high school equivalency through home study. Her mother had M.S. and went into a nursing home when Eileen was fifteen years old. She and her father visited her mother daily and took her out of bed with a hydraulic lift. Eileen was always good at art in school; after she moved to South Boston in 1981, she began painting and taking art classes. Eileen has been an active volunteer throughout her life and also rescues stray cats. She was president of an auxiliary for eight years.

JOSEPH R. SAIA has lived in South Boston since 1925. His father and mother came from Mineo, Sicily, Italy. He married his wife Carmella and they will celebrate their sixty-sixth year of marriage in August 2007. They have three children: two girls and a boy; eleven grandchildren; and four great-grandchildren. He and his brother Sal served in World War II and were proud to serve. He met Sal in Paris for three days during the war and they both came back to South Boston. "God Bless America, which we love."

BARBARA (BASIA) SIGNOR is seventy-three years of age and has kept herself busy since retirement. She has two sons and a daughter and has been blessed in being a grandmother and a great-grandmother. She volunteers as a teacher of knitting and crocheting. "I am a very wealthy woman—not in material things, but in the blessings God has given me. Wonderful family, wonderful friends, and the gift of passing on what I know to others."

MARION (GREEN) SMITH was born and raised in Roxbury, where for sixty years she has been a community activist. Widowed with a young son and daughter, Marion was determined to keep her kids on the right track and became involved in children's activities. When her son's Boy Scout troop was short an adult, she became a lady Boy Scout leader. Having been a bugler, she became a drill team instructor, then director of the girls' drum and bugle corps, the Cardinal Cushing Cadets, which won the CYO Championships nine years in a row and marched in local parades with eight consecutive mayors. Marion was inducted into the Massachusetts Drum Corps Hall of Fame.

LOUISE TAGLIERI is a lifelong Bostonian and has three daughters and two sons, ten grandchildren, and four great-grandchildren. Louise came down with empty nest syndrome at age forty-five and began her career as a clerk/typist. In due time, she became a social worker, serving proudly at the Boston City Hospital Department of Public Welfare for ten years, for which she received a citation from the Senate. Since retiring in 1992, she has traveled to over twenty countries, and leads a group to Sicily every fall. Louise is also active in her community, and serves as the President of the Ladies Society for the Madonna of the Caves annual North End festival, which has been held for eighty years.

ROSE TOSCANO has lived in the North End for more than eighty years. She has three brothers and three sisters. She raised three daughters and one son. Rose worked for twenty-eight years for the Sheraton Corporation in accounts receivable. When she retired she became involved in the community as president of the North End Younger Seniors, vice president of the Nazzaro Center board, member of the North End Union board, and attended many meetings when the Big Dig began. Although she still serves the seniors' group she says, "It is time for the younger generation to get involved!" Rose has eight grandchildren and six great-grandchildren.

ESTHER WILLIAMS was born near Youngstown, Ohio, in 1918. Her family moved to the Roxbury section of Boston in 1935, where she has lived ever since. Married in 1945, she and her husband bought a home and raised their two children. "I can't think of any place in the world I'd rather live."

# Suggested Reading

For further reading on these historic Boston neighborhoods, or for help in writing your own memoir or autobiographical essay, please consider these resources:

## NORTH END

Riccio, Anthony V. *Boston's North End: Images and Recollections of an Italian-American Neighborhood.* Essex, Conn.: Globe Pequot, 2006.

Puleo, Stephen. *The Boston Italians: A Story of Pride, Perseverance, and Paesani, from the Years of the Great Immigration to the Present Day.* Boston: Beacon Press, 2007.

Sammarco, Anthony Mitchell. *Boston's North End (Images of America).* Mt. Pleasant, S.C.: Arcadia Publishing, 2004.

## ROXBURY

Sammarco, Anthony Mitchell and Charlie Rosenberg. *Roxbury (Then & Now).* Mt. Pleasant, S.C.: Arcadia Publishing, 2007.

Sammarco, Anthony Mitchell. *West Roxbury (Images of America).* Mt. Pleasant, S.C.: Arcadia Publishing, 2004.

## SOUTH BOSTON

MacDonald, Michael Patrick. *All Souls: A Family Story from Southie.* New York: Ballantine Books, 2000.

Sammarco, Anthony Mitchell and Charlie Rosenberg. *South Boston (Then & Now).* Mt. Pleasant, S.C.: Arcadia Publishing, 2006.

WRITING

Franco, Carol. *The Legacy Guide: Capturing the Facts, Memories, and Meaning of Your Life*. New York: Tarcher, 2006.

Rainer, Tristine. *Your Life as Story*. New York: Tarcher, 1998.

Zinsser, William. *Inventing the Truth: The Art and Craft of Memoir*. Boston: Mariner Books, 1998.